The Stress-Less Baby Guide

Sarah Kaldor

First published by Busybird Publishing 2018

Copyright © 2018 Sarah Kaldor

ISBN   ebook - 978-1-925692-90-7

Print - 978-1-925692-59-4

Sarah Kaldor has asserted her right under the Copyright, Designs and Patents Act 1988 to be identified as the author of this work. The information in this book is based on the author's experiences and opinions. The publisher specifically disclaims responsibility for any adverse consequences, which may result from use of the information contained herein. Permission to use information has been sought by the author. Any breaches will be rectified in further editions of the book.

All rights reserved. No part of this publication may be reproduced, stored in or introduced into a retrieval system, or transmitted in any form, or by any means (electronic, mechanical, photocopying, recording or otherwise) without the prior written permission of the author. Any person who does any unauthorised act in relation to this publication may be liable to criminal prosecution and civil claims for damages. Enquiries should be made through the publisher.

Cover image: Rhian Awni

Layout and typesetting: Busybird Publishing

Busybird Publishing
2/118 Para Road
Montmorency, Victoria
Australia 3094
www.busybird.com.au

Disclaimer

Whilst I have sought to include the most accurate and up to date evidence on all topics in this book, I have also included some insight, personal opinions and wisdom from my clients and my own experience. I don't always stick to the rulebook, and as you will find as you embark on your journey, you probably won't either.

It would be remiss of me not to say that the information in this book should not replace the specific guidance of your own healthcare professional.

I am eternally indebted to my clients over the years who have shared their journeys with me, as well as my own babe Eliza, who patiently accepted me whilst I fumbled through my own first-time parenting experience.

Contents

About the Author	1
Getting prepared	3
Buying stuff	5
Birth	17
Your body after birth	21
Breastfeeding	27
Milk: how much, how often?	37
Bottle-feeding with formula or breast milk	43
Normal physical stuff that will happen to most babies	49
Poo	57
Development	59
Unsettled periods in newborn babies: wind and 'colic'	65
Your emotional wellbeing	69
Thinking about your relationships after baby comes along	77
Social support	87
Getting out of the house	91
Sleep	93
SIDS	105
Choosing your GP and meeting your health nurse	109
Growth	111
Immunisation	115
Dr Google	117
Introducing solid food	119
Food allergies	133
Teething	135
Safety	139
Illnesses and when to seek medical assistance	143
Leaving your child in the care of others and going back to work	145
Centrelink	149
Your better life as a parent	153
Reflections	155
Parent information helplines by state	157
Summary of website resources	160

About the Author

Sarah is a registered nurse, midwife, maternal and child health nurse and lactation consultant.

She lives and works in Melbourne with her husband Luke and daughter Eliza.

The recipe to surviving and enjoying your first year

Ingredients:

Get support

Have realistic expectations about what having a baby is all about

Learn to roll with the punches

Chant the parenting mantra: This too shall pass

Finished product:

A parent who stresses less

And is more able to enjoy their baby

xxx

Getting prepared

1) **Book in** - with a health care provider and birthing/parenting/breastfeeding classes.

2) **Start saving** - This baby stuff and having time off work is *expensive*!

3) **Learn** - This book is a quick reference of what's to come in terms of baby care, feeding, sleep, development and your wellbeing, with plenty of relevant online links and resources that can provide you more details about specific topics.

4) **Think about your village** - Who is going to support you and in what way?

5) **Buying stuff** - The fun bit!

Buying stuff

It would be impossible for me to try every baby product under the sun. If you want to get an idea of what the 'best product' is, there are plenty of reviews online. I can, however, speak a fair bit on what's practical for most people, and what's completely unnecessary (which should hopefully save you some dollars).

There are so many products out there that are always changing. The baby product industry is a multi-million-dollar industry and it is hard not to get sucked into spending thousands (I'm not joking!) on baby stuff.

I do believe that you can buy quality things without the thousand dollar price tags that come along with 'designer brands'. There are also plenty of things you can buy second-hand (#gumtreegeneration) that are safe and clean and will serve you just as well as something brand-new. The bottom line: don't put yourself under financial strain to buy everything new or designer.

But if you've got plenty of dough, enjoy yourself – baby stuff is so fun to buy!

A car seat and pram

Option 1: Baby capsule, 0-6 months.

Baby capsules can attach directly to most prams so you can transfer baby out of the car and clip him straight onto the pram.

Option 2: Permanent car seat, age 0-5 years.

Baby will need to be unbuckled and taken out of it when the car trip is done to transfer into a pram or into the house.

If you buy a capsule – you'll need to get a bigger car seat after six months or so. Many people borrow a baby capsule from friends or family since it gets used for such a short amount of time. I personally found our baby capsule to be a good investment as Eliza could fall asleep in the car and continue to sleep in the capsule once the car trip was done and we'd gone inside. Babies shouldn't routinely sleep in the capsule, but if you're keeping an eye on them, half an hour won't hurt.

If you don't buy a baby capsule, you will probably need a flat, bassinet-type connection for your pram for your newborn baby. The standard pram seat is marketed for the six-month-plus age group or when the baby at least has some neck control. I find babies that are around three months old hate lying flat in the bassinet bit because they are ready to look around and see the world. Once they have a bit of head control, you should be able to safely use the normal pram seat in a reclined position.

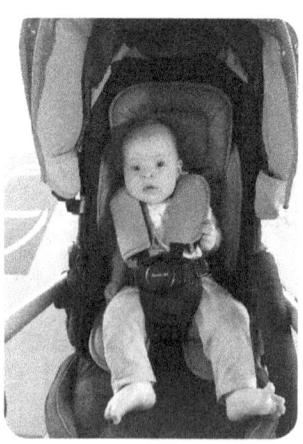

Little Miss Eliza, ready to graduate to her big girl pram at three months

A cot with/without a bassinet

Most babies grow out of their bassinet within about three months. Is it worthwhile for you to have one for that time? It might be, for example, if you'd like the baby to be in your room and the cot would never fit, or you have a double-storey house and want your baby sleeping downstairs in the first few months.

They are not super-cheap, so perhaps you could borrow one. Could you buy one on Gumtree and get a new mattress? My girlfriend had a Moses basket that I borrowed which was perfect for a house with stairs.

Later, we will talk about sleep environments being quiet(ish) and dark so we don't want baby napping in the overstimulating living room past about two months. Is it easy enough to just take your baby to their cot in their room for each sleep?

All cots bought brand-new in Australia should comply with the Sudden Infant Death Syndrome (SIDS) guidelines. If your cot is second-hand or from overseas, check out the Red Nose website: **https://rednose.com.au/**).

More on SIDS later.

Baby clothes

There is a very good chance you will receive a *lot* of clothes as gifts. If your baby is born over 3.5 kgs, she won't be in newborn sizes for long. Buy yourself enough onesies and singlets that, if your baby soils herself multiple times in one day, you will have time to wash and dry everything and still have a clothed baby. Then see what you get in terms of gifts.

Swaddles/sleep bags

The same goes for things like swaddles: you will probably be given so many. You will find your little wriggler won't stay contained in their swaddle in the way the hospital showed you for very long. Babies love having their hands up by their face, but they also have a 'startle' reflex which will wake most of them if you don't swaddle them. The easiest solution is to buy something like a Love to Dream swaddle **(Love to Dream swaddles https://lovetodream.com.au/)**.

Love to Dream is now a big *big* business. No surprises there. It is currently the most practical baby sleeping bag on the market! Love to Dream was created by an innovative mummy (#mumpreneur) who was on maternity leave and looking for a sleep solution for a baby who didn't like to be swaddled because he liked his hands up near his face. I wish I had invented that thing – genius!

Whichever sleeping bag you choose, there are lighter and heavier ones to accommodate the different seasons.

If you choose not to use a sleeping bag, your baby will need to clothed appropriately so he doesn't get cold. You might need to use a heater overnight.

Bottles, dummies, and formula

It is admirable to have the best intentions of exclusively breastfeeding your baby but don't leave yourself in a position where you're running out to the shops at midnight to try to find bottles, dummies or formula because your baby is starving and you are about to tear your hair out! I'd have at least one bottle and dummy and some sachets of formula in the cupboard just in case as a safety net. If you end up bottle-feeding more regularly, you can build up your stash of bottles when that happens.

I personally didn't buy any of these things with some kind of false sense of security or arrogance that I would exclusively breastfeed, but by the second night in hospital, I was calling my girlfriend for bottles and dummies!

Regarding dummy use, not all babies need a dummy. So have one on standby and wait and see. Some babies do seem to need extra sucking for comfort in-between feeds. Some mums are happy to use their breast for this; some babies learn to suck on their hands.

It's probably valid if you're worried about your baby getting too attached to a dummy, as lots do. But if they are babies who really need to suck, they will learn to suck their hands anyway. Hands will always be attached to their body and are harder to wean the baby off.

So, if you feel your baby really needs the extra sucking, don't stress about using a dummy. They might get over it in their own time. If they don't, you can trade it with Santa for something bigger and better once the child can understand.

Please note: excessive dummy use in the early months can interfere with milk supply.

Breast pumps

I wouldn't necessarily buy a pump outright before you know how your breastfeeding journey is going to go. It might end up being a total waste of money. I'd leave it or borrow one from someone for the first few weeks. If pumping becomes part of your routine, you can get some advice about what might be a good pump for you.

You can hire a hospital-grade pump from your hospital, a pharmacy or the Australian Breastfeeding Association (ABA). Medella is a great brand for breast pumps. Spectra are also well regarded and they make more affordable hospital-grade pumps that you can buy outright.

There are lots of perfectly good second-hand Medella and Spectra pumps for sale out there too. You will need to buy the plastic pump kit to go with it, which is the bit that comes in contact with your breast, the milk and your baby. Buying a second-hand breast pump and a new plastic pump kit is perfectly hygienic.

Whichever pump you choose, it is important that it has adjustable settings for both the speed and strength of the suction.

A breastfed baby will typically suck quickly and more softly for the first minute or two until the milk starts flowing and then change to a long and strong suck. Your pump should be able to replicate this.

If you look at a pump that costs less than $200 brand-new, it's probably going to be a bit of a dud. You get what you pay for in this department. So it might be worth considering spending a bit more, hiring one, buying one second-hand or borrowing one.

A bottle steriliser won't go astray and you can buy one that you put in the microwave (not electric) for about $50. A microwave steriliser requires a cup of water in the bottom, a minute or two in the microwave and, bang, the bottles are sterilised – the easiest and cheapest option.

Change table

Lots of people don't think they will need one until they realise how sore their back gets bending over the baby on the bed or the floor. Buying one that is combined with a set of drawers is a good option if you need a bit more storage for baby stuff. Alternatively, free-standing ones aren't super-expensive and are easily bought second-hand.

Many people will skip the change table all together and just put a towel on the couch or bed. Later, once the baby is rolling around, you might need to ditch the change table for nappy changes on the floor anyway.

Bath Stuff

Your average bath holds too much water for a little munchkin. You can buy a small plastic baby bath for about $30. It will take up room once you're not using it anymore but you can store toys in it and keep it for next time, or make a friend a baby hamper with it. Alternatively, use the laundry sink while the baby is small.

It can be pretty hard going on your back holding and supporting the baby the whole time they are in the bath. A few alternatives to doing this long-term are to put a non-slip mat on the bottom of the bath, fill it up a little and let the baby lie flat with a little towel under his head (it is fine for them to get a bit of water in their ears).

Or, once bubs has a bit of head control, you can buy a bath hammock that a baby can recline in, in bath bliss! They aren't that expensive either. Again, I borrowed one of these from a girlfriend.

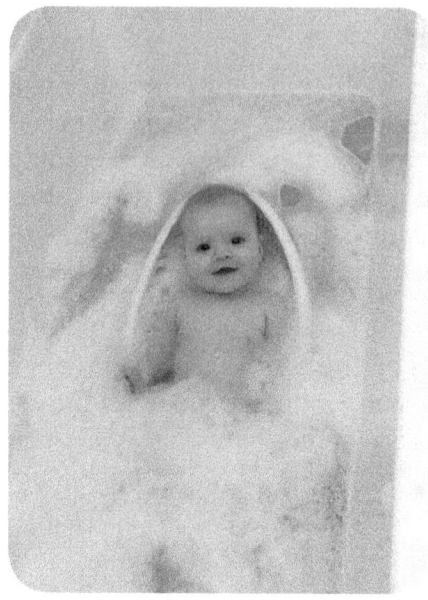

Eliza in her borrowed bath hammock

High chair

Don't bother looking at these until your baby is getting closer to solid foods. When he's nearly there, take him into the store to try some out and see what seems functional for you. Ease of cleaning is paramount. $25 at Ikea will give you an uber-functional, easily cleaned high chair.

Nappies

Disposable nappies make a huge imprint in our waste production and are therefore not great for the environment. If you feel like you could be bothered washing cloth nappy liners, give it a go. I bought some initially with the best intentions, but didn't follow through as I was too lazy, but many can and will. There are some really cute ones out there. After the initial investment, they don't work out to be more expensive, just a bit more work.

Old-school cloth nappies (the ones our parents used to put on us with a pin and soak in a bucket) are still available in baby stores and are great to put under your baby when your change them, under their head when they are sleeping (if they are pukers) or on your shoulder when burping.

Buying newborn bibs in bulk will also serve you well if you have a bit of a puker; it is so much easier to wash a bib or cloth nappy than to change a whole outfit or all the bedsheets.

Nappy Bin

It ends up stinking out your baby's room. It's gross. Straight into the big bin, I say!

Bouncer

I personally think these are a good investment and you don't need to spend much on them. Babies love to feel like they are being held, so being in a rocker which is a bit upright and vibrates a little might buy you a bit of time to have a cuppa. Don't spend $500 on that 'jumparoo' thing or $400 on the swinging leafy one – it won't work any better than your average $50 bouncer.

Breastfeeding chair

No, you don't need one of these. A good comfortable chair that supports your back will do. A footstool is also essential if you're a shorty like me.

Baby carriers

Baby carriers are not for everyone. Definitely don't buy one until you have your baby. Luke and I only ever used ours when we travelled and couldn't have our pram. Luke found it to be an extremely hot and sweaty exercise.

If you have a baby who is clingy and less likely to settle unless being held, using a carrier might be helpful for you when you're trying to get some things done.

Baby slings can cost a bit so I expect it would be a good to borrow one from a friend and see how you like it before investing. As with breast pumps, you get what you pay for. Don't buy a cheapy: it might not be supportive enough for your back and to position baby safely.

If you do end up using a sling, there should be a *very* clear guide on how to use it safely, particularly with newborn babies. There have been many devastating deaths of little ones who got smothered in their slings. Have a close look at this safety guide: **http://raisingchildren.net.au/articles/baby_slings_carriers_safety.html**

Baby monitor

I didn't buy one initially as I didn't think I'd need it, thinking I'd hear Eliza if she needed me. However, I felt my house was too small and noisy to leave her door open when she slept and I often woke her by sneaking in to see what she was doing. So we eventually caved and bought a monitor with a video function on it so we could spy on her. We have used it to death! We take it with us everywhere – enough said.

A note on sneaking around

Don't get in the habit of doing it. Luke and I are still tip-toeing around during nap time two years on!

Let your baby get used to a reasonable amount of background household noise while they sleep.

Birth

There is probably a bit too much hype about the birth itself, which, in reality, is a very short-term event compared to the long-term outcome – the baby. However, given that a lot of women feel a bit traumatised after the birth experience, it is important to be prepared and realistic about what you might go through. It would be awful if your negative feelings about your birth experience got in the way of you getting started with your parenting journey.

Time and time again I have come across women who tell me how woeful their hospital experience was or how terribly they were treated by staff, only to hear the story and think to myself, 'Wow, that sounds pretty standard to me!'

So, be informed about what the standard practices in your hospital are. Be prepared for what might happen to you. Go to the classes they provide. Ask questions. Tell your care provider what your wishes are.

I can't advocate highly enough for continuity of care in your pregnancy and knowing the person who will be caring for you during the birth. This is possible in both public and private care. In the public system, it'll be called something like caseload midwifery or midwife group practice. It's like having your own private obstetrician without the pay packet. It will be staffed by the most experienced and passionate midwives in that hospital. It is brilliant.

Your options for birth and pregnancy care might change, depending on where you live in Australia. For example, in more rural towns, your local GP or obstetrician might be the main person to see you through pregnancy and birth.

Starting with a local GP as your first point of call is the best way to find out all your options for pregnancy and birth care.

The Better Health Channel has a good fact sheet on this: **https://www.betterhealth.vic.gov.au/health/healthyliving/ pregnancy-care-choices**

If you prefer private care, this can be brilliant too. What I will say about obstetricians is that they make a certain amount of dollars for every baby they deliver, so naturally some obstetricians will book loads of women each month. The result is they are super-busy and could be more likely to induce you or give you a Caesarean section because this is more time-effective and predictable for them. Just make sure that, if you don't want that kind of scenario, your obstetrician is one who limits their number of monthly bookings and has respect for the way you hope to give birth and that they won't intervene needlessly.

Saying that, birth can be unpredictable, so it's not always that easy for health care providers to stick to 'birth plans' without compromising the safety of you and your baby. If you're lucky, the baby will come flying out. If you are like most first-time mothers, the first one paves the way and it can be a lengthy process. At times, the longer the process goes on, the more it requires a bit of medical intervention.

I had a 'burger with the lot' kind of birth: a IV drip, having my waters artificially broken, an epidural (my choice), foetal monitoring, a baby stuck in a weird position requiring forceps in theatre under spinal anaesthetic, a retained placenta, a massive haemorrhage and about a three-hour period of unconsciousness!

But, as a midwife with an understanding of the complexity of the birth process, I was not (mentally) traumatised by what we went through. I knew everything that was happening to me was guided by best practice and in the interests of the health of me and my baby. That's all you can ask for.

This is not a birth book, so we'll leave it at that!

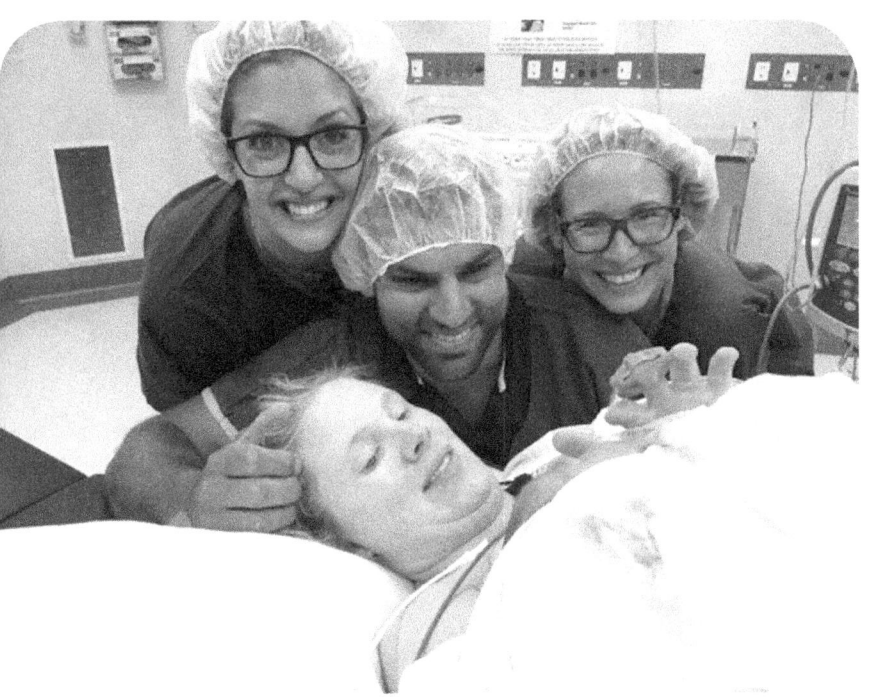

My 'burger with the lot' birth with Luke and my two beautiful caseload midwives, Serena and Mel

Your body after birth

Although I didn't find my 'all-inclusive buffet' birth emotionally traumatic, the physical aftermath was different. I thought I was ruined forever and would require all kinds of reconstructive surgery. I was not emotionally scarred but I was physically traumatised. Physical trauma is pretty common to some degree for most mums, particularly first-time mums.

Pelvic floor and continence

The pregnancy itself will stretch your pelvic floor muscles; this has implications for how you can control your bowel and bladder. A lot of women have a short-term loss of sensation of their pelvic floor directly post-birth.

On top of this, the hospital will often give you laxatives to help you poo when you have stitches (after a vaginal birth) or have been taking lots of pain medication (after a Caesar). Needless to say, my baby was not the only one needing nappies the week after giving birth.

Some women find it extremely traumatic to wet or soil themselves, so it's good to be prepared it might happen and that, for most women, it's a short-term problem. It'll get better with time, rest and pelvic floor exercises. If it doesn't, a women's health physiotherapist is your first port of call. Your hospital will usually have this kind of service. If you're concerned, get a referral before you leave the hospital.

Healing your stitches

Initially, it can be quite swollen down there, so rest is best. As much as you can, lie down. For the first few weeks, I had to either sit with a doughnut under my bum or lie down.

An ice pack to the area can help with swelling. I opted for a long icy pole that I crushed inside its packet so it was flexible and wrapped in an absorbent cloth. Lie with it between your legs for twenty minutes, then chuck the whole thing out. Beats buying a vaginal icepack that you have to wash and refreeze in between.

Anti-inflammatories are great for this kind of swelling as well as helping with any pain it might be causing.

As well as helping the swelling to go down, salt baths will help heal the skin itself. Try to have one every day if you can. Have a nice big bag of table salt in your pantry as part of your baby prep!

Your new vagina

A lot of women describe their post-birth vaginal anatomy as very different. Unfortunately, this is normal for most women. While it might look different, perhaps not so neat or compact, it will continue to serve the purpose it was designed for. Once all the swelling has gone down and the stitches healed, you can assess the damage and get to know your new vagina.

Your bum

Haemorrhoids, for most women – fun times! These might have developed in the pregnancy itself from the pressure of the baby on your pelvic floor.

Mine were apparent but not a huge problem in the pregnancy. After three hours of trying to push a baby out, they became a little (a lot!) more apparent. Now, maintaining my bowel habits is the only way of keeping them at bay. Constipation = haemorrhoids.

It is important that you don't allow yourself to get constipated in the first few weeks. There is nothing worse than feeling like you are giving birth to a poo baby in the weeks after giving birth to a real baby.

Some women find a bit of reassurance from folding up some toilet paper to support their stitches while they do a poo to stop the stitches from 'bursting'. (They wouldn't burst, by the way, but you might feel like that).

Keep up your fluids and your fibre and if you need to, take stool softeners. Your bowel habits will normalise once you stop taking strong painkillers and you are back to a relatively normal diet and a bit of activity.

Your body after caesarean section

Three words: **Major. Abdominal. Surgery.**

Anyone else who was having such a surgery would be resting in bed for days while being heavily medicated with painkillers. Meanwhile, new mums might get one night in bed and are up the next day, ready to learn how to care for baby. It's hard yakka and I take my hat off to you!

If you've had a Caesar, there is probably a bit more recovery for your body to do compared to a vaginal delivery. Although you didn't give birth vaginally, the pelvic floor stuff still stands.

Your abdominal incision will include interference to the

skin, muscle and uterus layers. The skin will heal most quickly, usually within a week or two, although infection of Caesar scars is quite common. If the site is really red, oozing, coming apart or smelly, get it checked. You might need antibiotics.

Not only has your pregnancy caused separation of your abdominal muscles, the doctors have physically moved them out of the way to get to your uterus. Many women have subsequent muscle strains or tenderness for weeks to come after a Caesar.

The whole thing can be pretty painful so it's no surprise that you'll probably need to take strong painkillers at least until you go home from hospital, if not for a few more weeks afterwards.

It'll be harder to do everyday stuff like showering, bending, lifting and so on, and you are likely to need some hands-on help at home for at least six weeks while your body recovers, especially if you have older children.

Ask for a physio review before you head home from the hospital; they should be able to give you some advice on how you can support the area while you are healing.

Bleeding

It is normal to bleed for about six weeks after birth. You should bleed less as the weeks go on, but you might find you have a bit of a gush when the baby feeds or you go for a walk. As long as it's slowing down in general and looking more like the end of your normal period, you're all good.

Lots of women will pass some clots; this is only as issue if there are lots of big ones (which would add up to a large volume of blood loss) or they are very smelly or look like bits of placenta or membranes. If you feel symptomatic of blood loss, are looking really pale or feeling faint you will need to call your obstetrician or hospital.

Abdominal separation and back pain

Your pregnancy has probably separated your tummy muscles to some degree; hopefully, one of the midwives or physios in the hospital will have checked this for you. Regardless, most women will have some weakness in their tummy muscles for a period of time after the birth and your back will generally compensate for this weakness. So, be *most* careful to support your back in every way possible until your stomach comes good.

Like I wrote earlier, ask for a physio review or class before you head home from hospital. They'll be able to give you some individual advice about how to support the area while it heals. Many clients and friends of mine use 'recovery shorts', which cost an arm and a leg, but people swear by them. I'll let you know if I try it next time!

Feeding and nursing a baby can cause some pain and stiffness in the neck and shoulders also. Once you get the hang of handling your baby, try to be mindful of this and relax your shoulders when you are feeding. Try to swap which arm you cradle the baby in so you're not always craning your neck in one direction.

Six-week postpartum check-up

Keep in mind you should have a postpartum check-up around six weeks after birth. This is enough time for the body to heal up and let you know if there are any ongoing issues that need to be addressed.

Your appointment should be with your GP or obstetrician. They can check your wounds, follow up with any blood tests that needs to be done, write you a script for contraception and book in your next pap smear.

Don't let them talk you into a pap smear at six weeks postpartum if you've had stitches down there; that's just crazy! Tell them you'll book back in a couple of months.

Sex after birth

This will fall into place eventually. Anyone who is breastfeeding will have a reduction in lubrication down there: lubricant is therefore your best friend. GPs can also prescribe oestrogen cream for the dry vagina.

If you've had a Caesar, it may feel comfortable a bit sooner down there but your tummy and back will probably have lost a lot of their flexibility through having such a big operation.

For those with stitches in their vagina, it can take a while. The stitches turn into a scar and the scar tissue is not stretchy like vaginal wall tissue. So anything rubbing past or stretching the scar tissue will feel bad!

Try when you feel up to it, and always use lubricant. If it's too painful, try again later. Most people will be starting to get back on track between three to six months. After this time, if you can't do it because of pain, check it out with your doctor.

Breastfeeding

Oh my goodness – breastfeeding! Be prepared for it to be a challenge!

Human bodies were made to feed human babies, so breastfeeding should be our baseline normal way to feed a baby. Unfortunately for some (including myself), it's not as simple as wanting and being willing to breastfeed.

My opinions on breastfeeding are heavily influenced by my own experience of the emotional *angst* caused by trying to breastfeed. Full disclosure: I am not adverse to a bit of formula. Call me 'unmidwifely' but as a mother who struggled to make 100% of the milk my baby required, the ability to use a bit of formula set me free.

As a maternal and child health nurse and lactation consultant, I am happy to support a woman as far as she wants to go with her breastfeeding journey, whether it be for two weeks or five years. I don't believe that breastfeeding should continue at the expense of the emotional wellbeing of the mother. (If you are not aligned with this way of thinking, it might be better to skip this chapter all together.)

Obviously, we know breast milk has its proven health benefits. These include, but are not limited to, infant mother bonding, a human milk protein easily digested by a human gut, immunological benefits and antibacterial properties, all of which feed into a reduction in certain health concerns in children and adults. Breast milk requires no preparation, comes out at the right temperature and you won't need to clean or sterilise any equipment.

At the same time, we know formula-fed babies grow and thrive. Formula these days is sophisticated enough to have the right balance of vitamins and minerals that a baby needs to grow.

So, my personal opinion on this one is, be informed about the benefits of breastfeeding and make an informed choice about whether you want to breastfeed or not, then try your best to do it.

Persevere for at least two months, even if you're having trouble. I have had so many mums bravely persist and go on to exclusively breastfeed. They are so thrilled they stuck with it, even if there were many ups and downs and tears along the way.

Before the baby arrives

Breastfeeding is one of the hardest parts of parenting in the first year and needs a lot of support and coaching for it to be successful. I highly recommend you do everything to educate yourself before the baby arrives.

Learn how to hold a baby in the right position, learn how to hold your breast in the right position, learn about when your milk should come in and what you should do when your nipples are damaged so that, if (when) all of that happens, it is a little less overwhelming.

Most birthing classes will include some sort of breastfeeding education. Some hospitals will offer purely breastfeeding classes while others can organise an antenatal appointment with a lactation consultant. Book in, book in, book in!

Have a look at the Raising Children Network. They have some great video demonstrations on different aspects of breastfeeding: **http://raisingchildren.net.au/breastfeeding_videos/newborn_breastfeeding_videos.html**

Expressing before baby arrives

I recommend you discuss antenatal expressing with your care provider, as it can be very useful to have a bit of your breast milk on stock if you get separated from your baby or your baby goes to special care. This can also be very helpful if you have a hungry baby who is destroying your nipples! I went into the hospital with 40 mls of expressed milk but used it up in three days!

When the baby is born

When the baby arrives, it is important from a hormonal perspective that you try to cuddle and feed him as soon as possible after the birth.

In a lot of cases like my own, babies and mums are separated. If you have a good care provider, someone should be encouraging your partner to be doing the skin-to-skin in this time instead and giving the baby some of your expressed breast milk.

Breastfeeding support: private and public hospitals

If you are in a private hospital, you should hopefully get to remain in hospital until your milk has come in, a crucial time when new mums need breastfeeding support. Private hospitals will often have a lactation consultant in a 'feeding' room throughout the day.

Make use of it for every feed! The more support you get, the better.

If you are in a public hospital, they boot you out pretty quickly, almost definitely before your milk comes in. You might need to be proactive in seeking out extra support.

When you feed, you should always ring for a midwife. If you are having issues, ask them to refer you to the lactation consultant on duty that day. She will have longer to sit with you through a whole feed than a ward midwife who may be too busy.

Before you leave the hospital, make sure you address any of the concerns you have about feeding. Make a 'feeding plan' with your midwife and ask for an appointment with the outpatients lactation consultants in the next week; it's free. If you end up not needing it, you can cancel it. Like I said, the more support the better.

Get your partner or support person to observe as many of your breastfeeding lessons as possible, with the hope they can support you when the professionals aren't there.

A public hospital should offer you a home-visiting midwife. The hospital midwife will usually visit you in your home two or three times.

Private lactation consultants in the community

There are also many private LCs in the community who you can employ privately. Some may offer a Medicare rebate. Your friends, family, GP or health nurse might be able to recommend one or you can look here for a local one: **http://www.lcanz.org/find-a-lactation-consultant/**

Mixed advice

In hospital settings, you will come across health professionals who have different ideas about things. Please, just take what works for you from each person and try not to get too overwhelmed.

Breast is best (?)

If you come across someone who is very pushy about breastfeeding and you don't feel comfortable with this, remind them that breastfeeding your baby is not the only thing that you are trying to learn as a new parent at that very moment.

HAPPY MUM IS BEST!

The most important thing for your baby is that you are well and happy enough to care for them, enjoy them and love them. If, after a reasonable period of persistence and support, your breastfeeding journey is hindering your ability to feel well in yourself and enjoy your baby, find someone to support you to find a happy medium between breastfeeding and formula feeding, or full formula feeding.

Common breastfeeding speed humps

I don't want to go into a vast amount of trouble-shooting with breastfeeding. Variations such as blocked ducts, mastitis and nipple thrush don't happen to everyone. If they do happen to you, you are going to have to seek out a health professional in person. Be aware that these issues can occur and, if you experience them, get some advice as soon as possible!

The best way to prevent nipple thrush and mastitis is to prevent your nipples from getting damaged. Broken skin allows germs to get inside the breast.

The best way to prevent getting mastitis and blocked ducts is to make sure you try to drain at least one breast per feed (that is, the breast feels full at the start and soft at the end). Monitor yourself for any sore spots and blockages and try to get baby or the pump to unblock them as soon as you can.

Nipple Damage

Most women will get some level of nipple damage in the first week, no fault of their own. The fact is that you and your baby haven't done it together before and it takes a lot of learning. This is why it is so important to have close supervision with all feeds while in the hospital in order to make sure your attachment is good to minimise nipple damage.

Make sure someone has checked the anatomy inside the baby's mouth to make sure there is nothing irregular that could cause persistent nipple pain or damage.

Having some nipple first aid on standby won't go astray either. I like Multi-Mams Nipple Compresses, Hydrogel Breast Discs or something similar. They are like healing

Bandaids for your nipples. Other easy ideas for healing nipples include a bit of expressed breast milk rubbed on the nipple and air-drying with a bit of sunshine. Lansinoh is glorified moisturiser for your nipples.

Breastfeeding sensations

Most mums will experience a strong stretching or dragging sensation on the inside of the breast during feeding, particularly with the first few sucks. This is normal but takes a bit of getting used to.

A lot of women will also experience the feeling of their 'let-down' when the milk starts flowing, like a sting, cramp or tingle. Some won't feel it at all.

Engorgement

Most women will go through a bit of engorgement when the milk first comes in around day three to five. This means that, as well as having an increased volume of milk in your breasts, they will also be swollen. They will feel like boulders. More fun times!

You can get through this time by:

1) **making sure you drain your breasts.** If your baby is having trouble attaching to your balloons, you will need to hand-express a little milk out to soften the tissue around your nipple so your baby can latch properly.

2) **helping your body to reduce the swelling in your breasts by not rubbing, massaging or heating your breasts excessively.** Use some cool compresses (this is what cool cabbage

leaves were used for in the past) and talk to your doctor or pharmacist about taking anti-inflammatories.

This phase is brief but a common time for women to get mastitis if not managed properly. If you are having trouble with this, call your health nurse or the Australian Breastfeeding Association (ABA).

Uneven milk production between breasts

Most women will find one breast seems to produce more milk than the other, that it looks and feels bigger or that the baby likes that one better. All totally normal.

For some of you, you might need to start the feed on the less productive breast while baby is hungry and keen to suck, then end on the more productive one when baby is getting crabby.

I've had a few mums exclusively breastfeed from only one breast.

Breastfeeding with a health condition or taking medication

There are very few conditions and medications that contra-indicate your wish to breastfeed. I have had a countless number of clients come in and tell me they are pumping and dumping because they are on, for example, antibiotics. Which is ludicrous in most cases. Unfortunately for some mothers, a well meaning but ill-informed health professional might recommend pumping and dumping, 'just to be safe.' This is often without thought to the implications that this might have on your breastfeeding journey.

If you have a health condition, are on medication or have been told by a health professional not to breastfeed, your best chance of getting the absolutely correct information is to speak to a pharmacist in a maternity hospital who has specialised knowledge in breastfeeding or a GP who is also a lactation consultant.

Here is a list of informed persons in each state:

https://www.breastfeeding.asn.au/bfinfo/drugs.html

Milk: how much, how often?

When you leave the hospital, you might be on a fairly rigid feeding regime that your midwives or paediatrician have recommended. You might be feeding, for example, every three hours, whether the baby is crying for it or not. They might have told you to feed for a certain amount of time on each breast or a certain amount of milk in the bottle.

This is fine. Stick with this until you either meet your health nurse who can give you some more guidance as your baby grows and gets hungrier or, if you have a healthy, normal-sized baby, you might start to recognise that your baby's needs are changing and simply adapt to these new needs.

For example, they might feed more efficiently, so not want to feed for thirty minutes on each breast. Once your milk comes in, they might only want one breast per feed. They might want a feed after an hour or not want a feed for another four hours.

Once your baby is back to his birth weight, is having lots of wees and poos and is not jaundiced, it's probably time to ditch the rigid feeding schedule that the hospital sent you home with. Healthy babies have healthy appetites and can tell you when they are hungry. They are also safe to go longer periods without a feed if they wish.

Breastfeeding frequency

Your average baby will have six to twelve feeds in a twenty-four-hour period. As with everything, their needs are individual.

Most breastfed babies will feed *way* more than six times a day, especially when they are younger.

Breast storage capacity

Most women find that the amount of milk in their breast fluctuates throughout the day. For example, they have an abundance of milk in the morning, so maybe baby will only need to drink from one breast. By the afternoon, they feel that there is less milk in each breast; the baby definitely needs both sides and will even need to feed more often in the afternoon or evening.

This is a completely natural pattern of milk supply; it doesn't mean you don't have enough milk. It simply means that in those times of lower milk storage, you will need to feed more often for baby to get his fill. This is typically called 'cluster feeding'.

Signs your baby is getting enough milk

Breastfeeding is a bit of an art form. You will need to learn to trust your body. Observe if your baby is content, weeing and pooing a lot, sleeping for some stretch of time and growing.

If all that is happening, you are doing so, *so* well!

If you are demand-feeding your breastfed baby and they don't seem to be producing many wet nappies, they are not content or not growing; you will need to seek further breastfeeding support.

Most women are capable of making the full quota of milk for their babes, while a few, who have physical reasons why they can't, will need supervision by GP and a lactation consultant.

The art of milk supply

Your milk supply is regulated by your baby's demands; for most women, it is as simple as feeding your baby as often as they like to make enough milk.

To boost your supply, you might pump a bit in between feeds to send your body a message that the baby is drinking even more. Saying this, extra pumping might be a lot of work if you are already feeding your baby frequently.

On top of making sure you drain your breasts frequently, some might build their supply through the use of galactagogues. These are substances that can be found in both natural products such as foods and herbs as well as medications.

Most health food shops sell herbal tablets as well as breastfeeding 'cookies' or 'teas' that claim to support milk supply. They usually contain herbs such as fenugreek and blessed thistle or contain foods such brewer's yeast and oats – all goodies that can help some women produce more milk naturally.

A GP with a good knowledge of breastfeeding might also be able to prescribe a medication if they feel this could help you.

For more information, please refer to this page from the Australian Breastfeeding Association: **https://www.breastfeeding.asn.au/bfinfo/galactagogues-substances-claimed-increase-supply**

Your diet and breastfeeding

Don't get caught up in any of the dietary restrictions that people may suggest will make your baby less 'unsettled'. As we will discuss later in this book, colicky behaviour is part of the newborn phase. If your baby is going to be unsettled, they just will be, regardless of what you eat.

If you eat healthy balanced diet, your breast milk will be absolutely fine. Women with a vegan diet should have a consultation with a dietician, as a lack of animal products causes deficiency in some vitamins.

You should observe the same precautions with fish intake as you did in your pregnancy, recognising that if you had several serves of fish with a large mercury content in one week, this could cause unsafe levels of mercury in your breast milk.

You can resume eating the foods that have the potential to carry listeria, such as soft-serve ice cream, deli meats, soft cheese and pre-packaged salads. You are less susceptible to listeria now you aren't pregnant and immunocompromised.

Salty, sugary and spicy

Any foods consumed in excess may have the potential to make baby a bit more unsettled. For example, if you had a huge amount of caffeine, sugary food, salty food, spicy food or deep fried food in one sitting, this might be reflected in your breast milk. Anything in moderation will be absolutely fine.

Allergy to breast milk

Occasionally, some babies are truly allergic to something in your diet, such as dairy products. These babies would be awfully unsettled, typically have eczema and not grow very well. In this kind of setting, you and your health care provider would obviously know something is not quite right and your GP would refer you to a paediatrician for more guidance.

Alcohol and breastfeeding

You can certainly have a sneaky vino while breastfeeding if you time it carefully.

Have a look at the Australian Breastfeeding Association fact sheet: **https://www.breastfeeding.asn.au/system/files/ ABA_Alchohol_BF%2520for%2520website.pdf**

You can also download the 'Feedsafe' app.

Typically, it takes about one hour for an average woman to eliminate one standard drink from their blood stream. Your blood alcohol content will be reflected in your breast milk. Once you can guarantee that your baby won't need a feed for at least an hour, you can have one standard drink.

As your baby's sleep is more predictable (for example, when they sleep through the night), you could have a few drinks in the evening and be confident that it would all be out of your system in the morning.

If your breasts are uncomfortable earlier than the one hour per standard drink rule, you will need to pump and dump.

Keep in mind that your baby will probably still need you overnight, so if you plan on getting smashed, have someone else responsible for the care of the baby overnight. Hangovers are not conducive to parenting, so getting smashed will probably be a rarity or a thing of the past anyway.

Bottle-feeding with breast milk or formula feeding

Bottle-feeding is a bit more of a science as you can see exactly how much your baby is drinking. Some families find this incredibly reassuring. If you prefer to pump your milk out and give it in a bottle, that is your prerogative. It's a little bit more work and sometimes your milk supply doesn't maintain itself quite as well, but it's still a viable option.

Eliza cracked it with breastfeeding around the ten-week mark. My supply was dwindling because I was struggling to get her to stay on the breast for long enough and I was super-stressed out about it. I decided to pump and that turned out to be easier and less stressful for both of us. So, to each to their own.

Positives of bottle-feeding

There are a few perks to having a bottle-fed baby or at least a baby who can take a bottle from time to time. It gives mum a bit more freedom to move, literally, or sleep.

Breastfed babies often link breastfeeding to comfort so, for some mums, the feeding and the settling is all on her. I found that once Eliza was on the bottle, my hubby became proficient in all baby care, as he was able to do everything that I could do.

I'm not saying, 'Don't breastfeed' – I really wish I could have continued to feed Eliza beyond ten weeks and I hope to have more success with our next baby – but there are certainly some positives to bottle-feeding for some families. Again, to each their own.

Negatives to bottle-feeding

Bottle-feeding takes preparation and there is more risk of growth of bacteria in this process. You'll be doing a lot of washing and sterilising of equipment and it's harder to do when you're out and about.

Volumes

Bottle-fed babies will have relatively small volumes in the first week and then build up to something that resembles 150 mls of milk per kilo of baby per day for the first three months.

150 mls x baby's weight in kg x 24-hour period – that is, a 3 kg baby will drink somewhere around 450 mls in 24 hours. If they fed 8 times a day, that'd be about 55 mls per feed.

If you are giving formula, the tin will guide you. Like everything, it is only a guide. Don't stress if your baby's intake is slightly higher or lower than the calculation on the formula tin. If your baby is demanding more than the tin says, please don't stress that you are overfeeding him. If he is hungry, feed him. Just don't force him to finish the milk that's left in the bottle once he's had enough.

Most kids will get as far as about 180 mls per bottle at a time and that's as much as they can drink in one go. Some will always have smaller, more frequent, feeds; others will be able to drink 250 mls in one go! It's all good; let your baby dictate the amount.

Choosing a formula

There is such an overwhelming selection of formulas on our shelves these days. Luckily, for us in Australia, our formula production is strictly regulated and although there are a multitude of brands and different 'types' of formulas, they all have to have the right amount of vitamins and minerals, fats, proteins and carbohydrates that your baby needs. Effectively, any formula that you can buy on our shelves is fine.

Formulas with bells and whistles

Each formula company will have a variety of different kinds of formula products. I believe anything above the normal basic formula is a bit of a gimmick.

The ones with 'gold' in the title generally have some kind of added pre- or probiotic. The ones with HA (hypoallergenic) tend to be partially hydrolysed or whey-dominant formulas, designed to more closely mimic the composition of breast milk. On reflection from talking to families about formulas over the years, I find my clients more commonly complain their infant doesn't seem to 'agree' with these types of formulas with special extras.

Alternatives to cow's milk formulas

Most formulas are made from cow's milk. You might be aware there are other things out there, such as soy formula and goat's milk formula. There is no need to start with these kind of formulas and they are not recommended under the age of six months unless specifically directed by a paediatrician.

Soy is an alternative for when infants are allergic to cow's milk protein – but soy is a common allergen too.

Goat's milk formula is not nutritionally superior and not proven to be more easily digested, but is more expensive.

If your baby really struggles with your average formula for some reason, you probably need to get professional advice about where to go next with their formula.

Early bottle exposure in breastfed babies

It is not recommended to introduce any artificial teat such as dummies or bottles to a breastfed baby in the early weeks. The theory is that artificial teat use will interfere with the babies' ability to attach well to the breast. Sucking on a dummy might reduce the amount of time a baby spends at the breast, thus interfering with the mother's milk supply.

While this is all valid, a baby that never has a bottle might end up being a baby who utterly refuses to take one in the future. This can be difficult for mothers who need a break, need some time away or need to go back to work. If you feel you are going to be the kind of person who will need to be able to leave your baby for a period of time for any reason, you might want to think about the bottle becoming a semi-regular occurrence to keep your baby familiar with it.

Once you are comfortable that your breastfeeding is going well, perhaps your partner could give a bottle in the evening when you have a bit of a rest or a nice bath.

If you want to give your own milk, most women will find the morning time the best time to express some extra milk after the breastfeed. If you can only express a bit, maybe you could accumulate enough for one bottle every three days. Or you could give a bottle of formula. Whatever works!

Storing expressed milk and sterilising equipment

If you do express milk, you'll need to know how to store it hygienically. Check out this ABA fact sheet: https://www.breastfeeding.asn.au/bf-info/breastfeeding-and-work/expressing-and-storing-breastmilk

Pump equipment can be washed in between pumping sessions with warm soapy water, or not washed but kept in the fridge between pumping sessions. Sterilise it once a day.

Bottles that come in contact with formula will need to be sterilised each time.

Sterilised equipment can be kept in a sealed plastic container in the fridge and will stay sterile for twenty-four hours. For more information on formula hygiene and sterilising equipment, please refer to the Raising Children Network: **http://raisingchildren.net.au/articles/bottle-feeding_babies_equipment_formula.html**

Normal physical stuff that most babies will have

Newborn rash

Babies can be quite unsightly in the first few weeks. Lots of them have peeling skin, others develop a red pimply rash on their face and chest. This is called newborn rash and it's harmless if your baby is otherwise well.

To best manage their skin, make sure they are regularly moisturised with gentle non-fragranced skin care products; this will maintain their skin integrity. Dry skin cracks and lets in germs, which will make a rash worse.

Make sure they are not too hot and that their clothing is breathable; increased blood flow to the skin (when babies are too hot) will make a rash worse.

Babies need about one extra layer compared to what your average person is wearing. Not you, however: if you are breastfeeding and hormonal, you will generally be running hotter than your average person.

Belly buttons

The umbilical cord should fall off around a week after the baby is born. Don't pull it off, even if it's hanging by a thread. Lots will ooze or bleed a bit when the cord first falls off, then dry up on their own.

As long as the skin around the site isn't red, swollen or smelly, it's not infected. You could simply leave it to sort itself out or clean it with some salt water and give it some air time to dry. Belly buttons that continue to ooze for weeks might need cauterising with a bit of silver nitrate by your GP.

Nappy rash

Most people don't realise that a lot of nappy rash is caused by baby wipes, particularly if they contain a chemical called methylisothiazolinone (MI). If your baby is getting a sore bum, try ditching the baby wipes for a wet absorbent cloth or cotton balls.

A poo that is left for a prolonged period can also eat away at their sensitive skin, so try and change a pooey nappy as soon as you know it's there (unless they are asleep!). At night time, if they are going longer periods between feeds, use a barrier cream to protect their skin from developing a rash in the first place.

Once the rash has occurred, a thick layer of zinc cream with each (frequent) nappy change and some nappy-free time should heal it. If you don't see any improvement with the use of frequent nappy changes and a thick layer of zinc cream, take a photo and check it with your health nurse or pharmacist.

Orange and red stains in the nappy

Some babies will pass urates, which is basically extremely concentrated wee, in the first few days. This is completely normal.

Once they are getting plenty of milk through their system, this should go away. A little bit of bloody discharge from a baby girl's vagina in the first week is completely normal and is called a 'pseudo-period', which is simply a response to the withdrawal of mum's hormones that she was exposed to in the womb.

Show your midwife at the hospital if you see anything colourful in your baby's nappy.

Vomiting

So common. People will call this 'reflux' but, for most, it is just an overflow of milk. Babies have a very weak sphincter muscle at the top of their stomach that doesn't do a very good job at holding the milk in when their tummy is full. So the milk just overflows – voilà, baby vomit!

If the baby is not distressed by the vomiting and still growing well, it is simply more laundry for you. (Sorry, everyone!) Buy cloth nappies in bulk and use them wherever you go.

Baby will vomit less when the stomach muscle gets stronger and they start eating some food (around six months for most babies).

If your baby projectile-vomits frequently or seems very distressed when vomiting, discuss this with your health care provider.

Hiccups

Another product of digestive immaturity and *so* normal. Some babies get them more than others. You might be able to predict if your baby is going to be prone to hiccups if they had them frequently in utero. Hiccups generally just happen because their tummy is full and the muscles of their diaphragm are getting irritated. Nothing to be done about hiccups; don't worry about it.

Birth marks

Babies can be born with a variety of different spots and colours on their skin. Most of them are normal. The most common are the light red blotches on the eyelids, scalp and neck; these are called stork marks. They fade over time.

If your baby has a colourful spot that isn't a stork mark, take a photo and show your nurse/GP. Very occasionally, birth marks need more looking into.

Soft spot on top of the head (fontanelle)

Babies have four main skull bones that are not fused at birth in order to allow their head to be born through the birth canal and allow their brain to continue to grow to full capacity once they are earthside. This is also why lots of babies are born with funny shaped heads: after passing through the birth canal, the bones have crossed over each other! The fontanelle is essentially the soft tissue that connects these bones. Your baby will continue to have a 'soft spot' on top of their head for the first year or so. You don't need to do anything special to manage this soft spot.

Burping

A burp is simply a bit of gas that is produced in the stomach as a result of the process of digestion.

Bottle-fed babies may also gulp a bit of air during their feeds whereas breasts don't have any air in them!

To burp your baby, they need to be in an upright position so that, if there is gas in their stomach, it will rise. On your lap or over your shoulder – whatever feels comfortable.

Some people find their baby needs a bit of a burp during the feed. However, if they don't seem squirmy or uncomfortable, try not to disturb the rhythm of their feed. Once they are done, give them about five or ten minutes in an upright position to allow them to burp if they need to.

Don't stress if no burp happens in this time; this simply means there is no gas in their tummy. If they seem squirmy and uncomfortable later, perhaps you could sit them up or pop them back on your shoulder to see if they have developed some gas after digesting their feed.

Cradle cap

Cradle cap occurs in most babies and is a result of an overproduction of oil on the scalp. It isn't a big deal and, if there's only a little bit, don't worry about it. They grow out of it in the second half of the year.

If the cradle cap gets really thick, it can cause problems with itching, breaking the skin and even infection. If it is looking really thick and unsightly, get some advice on how to minimise it.

I used a bit of oil to soften the crust before bath time, gave it a gentle scrub in the bath, then combed it out the best I could with a very fine comb. Just be careful not to break the skin in the process.

Sticky eyes

Babies are more prone to sticky eyes in the early weeks – there are a lot of new germs in the outside world for them to adjust to after being in a sterile environment for nine months (the womb). If it is just a bit of discharge, clean them with salt water or breast milk. If the eye itself starts to get red or swollen, get your pharmacist or GP to check.

An eye that weeps with clear fluid is generally a blocked tear duct, which will only need medical intervention if it persists beyond the first year.

Eye colour and vision

You won't be able to tell your baby's eye colour for sure until the second half of the year, although you will get a pretty good idea about whether they will be on the lighter or darker side from birth.

From birth, babies can start to focus at short distances such as the distance between your faces when you are having a little chat.

They will see things in the distance as more of a blur, so will be more drawn to the contrast of light and dark, such as a ceiling light or a window. It takes a little while for their little eyes to start working together, so if you notice some crossed eyes, don't stress. Around six months, their eyes start working together, at which time they develop depth perception, things come much more into focus and colour vision becomes as sensitive as an adult's.

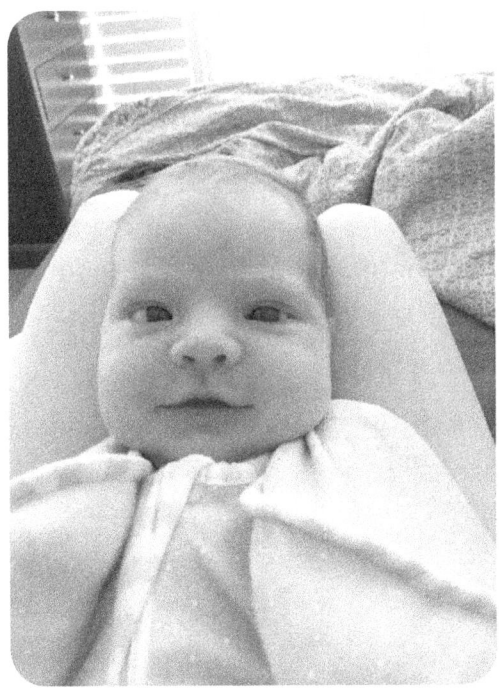

Eliza's googly Eyes at two weeks old. Note the stork marks on her upper lip, and the Love to Dream swaddle

Caring for little penises

In a western world of running water and daily baths, you really don't need to do anything specifically to keep your little boy's penis clean. Foreskins are not retractable at this age (not until two to three years) and you shouldn't try to force it back to clean under it.

Have a look at the Royal Children's Hospital fact sheet here: **http://www.rch.org.au/kidsinfo/fact_sheets/Penis_and_ foreskin_care/**

Caring for little vaginas

This might be a little daunting to begin with. Once you do it, day in day out, you'll get used to it! No rocket science to cleaning a baby's vagina. Vaginas are self-cleaning from the inside so you don't need to get all up in there, if you know what I mean. Clean away any poo you can see, wipe front to back to avoiding spreading more poo around her vagina. Give her a bath every day. That's about it!

You can also refer here:

http://raisingchildren.net.au/articles/baby_genitals_ cleaning_care.html

Poo

I spend a lot of my day talking to people about baby poo. It is weird and wonderful and can vary in an amazing amount of ways! Let's explore…

Colour

Your baby's poo will be black for a few days. Once they start to get a bit of milk through their system, it will change to a dark green and finally to full milky poo colour – which might be any shade of yellow, green or brown. It shouldn't continue to be black. It should never be white or red.

Texture

Breastfed baby poo will often seem like diarrhoea, it may have little seed-like lumps in it – all normal. Formula-fed baby poo might be more pasty. Baby poo shouldn't be hard or pebbly.

Frequency

How often doesn't really matter. It might range from every nappy change for some babies to once every ten days for others. Unless the poo is hard and difficult to pass, the baby is not constipated.

Saying this, lots of babies will be cranky and uncomfortable if they go for an extended period of time without a poo.

If you think this is the case, have a chat to your nurse/pharmacist/GP about how you might help them to go a bit sooner or make them a bit more comfortable.

Development

It's hard not to compare your baby with other babies, especially when it comes to development but, in this department, comparing is most certainly a waste of energy. The range of 'normal' is vast for most developmental milestones. For example, some babies will start to crawl as early as five months; some won't crawl until their birthday. Some babies will smile for the first time at two weeks old; some won't smile for months. Most end up reaching the same milestones but in their own way and their own time, so try not to compare.

For a rough guide of when babies should reach key milestones, have a look in your child's health record or look up the Raising Children Network Development Tracker: **http://raisingchildren.net.au/development/babies_development.html**

Babies who are late to reach milestones

If you're concerned your baby is not on track, start by having a look at what the normal age range for developing that milestone is. You may be surprised that your child is nowhere near the upper limit of normal and still has plenty of time to achieve it.

Some babies will progress quickly in one area of their development while falling behind in others and this is completely normal. For example, Eliza was very early to develop language (taking after her mother there!) while was very slow to crawl (not until after her first birthday).

If in doubt, have a chat to your health nurse, GP or paediatrician. A lot of the time, babies just need more time or opportunity to develop and you might get some ideas about how to facilitate your child's learning. Occasionally, children can't develop their milestones for a reason. For example, a child's speech might be delayed because they can't hear properly or your child can't learn to crawl because they have hated tummy time and barely spent any time on the floor. Your health nurse or GP should be able to check for physical or environmental causes and refer you on to the appropriate allied health service who could assess the concern with specialised knowledge and expertise.

Some of the clever chickies in my mothers' group sitting up independently at around eight months. Note my girl on the right needing support to sit for the photo: Eliza was always the slowest to 'move' in our mothers' group despite being the eldest girl.

System overload

Babies go through so much growth and so many developmental milestones through the first year. They have to be born, learn to eat and digest, get approximately six teeth, learn to eat solid food, learn to move around and communicate with us.

You can imagine how busy their little brains are through the first year. Naturally, this can be a bit unsettling for them at times and they can have some fussy periods around big leaps in their development. A great resource to get your head around this phenomenon is The Wonder Weeks book/app: https://www.thewonderweeks.com

My mum literally scoffed out loud when she'd heard about this concept of an app telling us that our baby is due for an unsettled period – I agree; it is a very Gen Y approach to parenting – but the app is based on a book written by neurodevelopmental scientists who did years of research on thousands of children to find patterns of unsettled behaviour that was reflected in most children. The app is a quick reference of the timing and cause of 'wonder weeks' without having to do too much reading.

I used the app in Eliza's first year to make myself feel better when she was being very fussy/unsettled. 'Oh, it's a 'wonder week'; your little brain is going through a lot of change so you'll probably have a wonderful new skill next week.'

Priceless for new parent

The take-home message is that babies will have ratty periods through their first year (and probably the entirety of their second year, but let's not get ahead of ourselves!). It is good to be realistic about this and not too blindsided by it. It'll be more manageable and less upsetting to you if you know its normal, you know it's coming and 'this too shall pass'.

> *A word on challenging periods and behaviours*
>
> *Every age has its challenges and its beautiful bits. Even once they are young adults, they will stress you out and challenge you.*
>
> *So, if you think of it in this way, there is no point in wishing away a certain age and thinking to yourself 'once this is finished, it'll be easier'.*
>
> *Enjoy the beautiful bits in each age and try to accept that the difficult bits will pass…to become different difficult bits!*

Activities with your baby

I think we put a lot of pressure on ourselves to do lots of 'activities' with our babies because we feel we need to provide our children with all the opportunities they need to thrive and succeed. A lot of parents go a bit overboard with it.

Here's what your baby actually needs in the first year to develop normally:

You: they need you to be as happy and healthy as possible and for you to be enjoying them.

A chat: they need the people in their village to have a chat with them. It doesn't need to be about rocket science, just everyday reciprocal conversation. Books, rhymes and songs are a great way of starting off your baby's language development.

Some things to look at: for example, each day you might go outside for some fresh air or a walk. You might lie them under a dangly mobile that they can look and swipe at while you are making dinner.

Tummy time: to learn to develop neck control, to roll, and to crawl.

Their hands: as they get a bit older and can grasp objects, they will need access to their hands. Ditch the mittens, let them put stuff (within reason) in their mouth.

It is not necessary to sign your baby up to expensive gymnastics or music classes. However, if they enjoy it, you're happy to get out of the house and you can afford it – great. But don't force yourself to do these things because you think you *have* to do it for your baby to develop normally.

If you have the time and interest, watch the documentary

'Babies'. It follows four babies born in completely different physical, social and cultural environments in Mongolia, Africa, Japan and USA. They show how these babies are raised and how they all go through the identical pattern of normal development. It is stunning to see and reinforces the message that babies don't need a lot of toys or structured activities.

Toys

Toys are great but not hugely necessary. What kids love most is a cardboard box or to open all your drawers and pull out your kitchenware.

Rice in a jar = a toy.

Plastic spoon and bowl = a toy.

Keep it simple and don't break the budget buying stuff they will lose interest in in two weeks' time.

Borrowing toys from friends or toy libraries are a great way to save money on toys that your baby will get bored of quickly.

Find Australian Toy Libraries on the internet: http://www.toylibraries.org.au/

Outdoor play is literally priceless.

As long as babies have attentive caregivers and a safe environment to explore, they'll be fine. What you do above and beyond that is totally up to you!

Unsettled periods in newborn babies: wind and 'colic'

Unsettled behaviour will be evident in most of your newborn babies to some degree in the first few months. For the sake of ease of reading, I'll call this unsettled behaviour 'colic'.

Babies are born immature, including their gastrointestinal systems. They go from not having to digest anything other than a little bit of amniotic fluid to having a belly full of milk that they have to hold in their little stretched tummy, digest and finally poop out. It's the biggest transition a baby makes in the first few months and it takes a lot of getting used to. Babies will burp, spit up, grimace and grunt, pull up their legs, fart and poo.

It's normal. After a few months, they get used to these feelings of digestion and, while they will still digest and poo, they won't make such a big performance of it.

If they are unsettled and screaming around the clock or they don't start to grow out of it, there might be something more sinister going on, behaviour that may need further investigation by a paediatrician.

Go with your gut (pardon the pun) if you are concerned about your baby's digestion. If you go into the newborn period with realistic expectations of normal unsettled behaviour and you feel what is happening in your case is concerning, it's worth looking into further.

> *As with anything in your parenting journey, if you discuss your concerns with a health professional who tells you there's nothing wrong with your baby and you don't feel reassured, talk to another one. Parental intuition is very accurate when it comes to recognising that there is something not quite right.*

Temperament

Babies are born with their own little personalities; this will play into how they cope with this newborn phase, as well as other challenges throughout their childhood. You will get a sense very early of what kind of personality your baby has, whether they seem pretty calm and placid, are very easily upset or somewhere in the middle. Understanding and accepting your child's temperament will help you to be less stressed by their unsettled behaviour.

I call the really highly-strung little infants 'orchid babies' because they need a lot of special TLC to grow and thrive, but the effort is so worth it. I reassure my parents that these beautiful yet difficult babies seem to turn into the brightest little toddlers. So don't despair if you have a sensitive little sausage; there is beauty in every type of personality.

Managing the crying baby

In the beginning when your baby is crying and you are unsure why, you might like to start with this checklist: **http://raisingchildren.net.au/verve/_resources/crying_baby_file.pdf**

Managing colic

There are many different remedies out there for the treatment of colic, most of which have been studied and proven to have been merely a placebo. People will suggest things like herbal teas, wind drops and boiled water. They are unlikely to genuinely help your baby but in very small doses given as directed, they are not likely to be harmful.

Parental comfort measures such as cuddles, deep warm baths, baby massage and bicycle leg exercises are the only scientifically proven things to help your baby with their 'colic'. The Royal Children's Hospital have some wonderful fact sheets about a variety of different children's conditions. Here's the one on colic: http://.rch.org.au/kidsinfo/fact_sheets/Colic_crying_babies_unsettled_babies_Parent_handout/

If your baby likes to be held a lot, you might make your life easier by using a baby carrier. At least you can have your arms free and your baby will be happy because they are close to your body and in an upright position.

Some families might also consider alternative therapies such as a paediatric physiotherapist, osteopath or chiropractor who may identify some misalignment of the musculoskeletal system after the pregnancy and birth.

Eliza was pretty dreadful with 'wind' pains for the first three months, particularly at night time and after a feed. She needed to be held in a certain position, with her legs drawn against her chest, to feel comfortable for about an hour after a feed. I'll admit, Luke and I tried many of the remedies that come under the 'there's no evidence' category, purely out of desperation to do something! This included herbal wind drops made by a local naturopath, the occasional concoction to help her poo and a visit to the chiropractor.

Babies grow out of 'colic' around the third month. After that time, their crying becomes more predictable and easy to respond to. They will mostly cry when they need a nappy change or a feed and they don't seem to cry 'just because' anymore. Hallelujah!

Your emotional wellbeing

It is normal to feel like you're on an emotional rollercoaster after giving birth to a baby. The 'baby blues' don't even begin to cover the range of emotions a new parent might go through, particularly the parent who gave birth and is therefore also hormonal. Many women cry, at the drop of a hat.

I was really surprised with how hormonal I was after the birth of Eliza. I was an anxious wreck, everything overwhelmed me. I felt smothered by my baby. I catastrophised about the condition of my body.

The hormonal fog lifts at different times for different women but shouldn't go on for months. If it does, you probably need further emotional support. The Perinatal Anxiety and Depression Australia (PANDA) is a great organisation for this: http://www.panda.org.au/. Similarly, you might discuss it with your health nurse or your GP. In different states, they will have different counselling services, peer support groups and programs to support you.

Postnatal depression

Everyone has heard of postnatal depression. Statistically, one in seven women will suffer from postnatal depression and one in ten dads. I'd like to believe that we've come a long way understanding this and that there is much less stigma associated with it. As a result, partners and family members are better at identifying this in women and are more proactive in seeking more support for them. At some point, your health care provider should at least ask you, if not screen you, for PND. So that's great.

Most women will need additional support to get through PND, whether it be counselling, medication, and admission to a mother baby unit or all of the above. If you end up with PND, you must not battle through it. The most important thing for your baby is to have parents who are well and able to love and care for them. PND gets in the way of your ability to enjoy your baby.

Postnatal depression in dads and partners

Be aware, partners of women with PND are likely to be suffering with depression too. I hope we are getting better as a community in valuing our dads and their emotional wellbeing as well. If you're worried about dad, this website by PANDA might be a good starting point: **http://howisdadgoing.org.au/**

Postnatal anxiety

Anxiety is more common and more commonly recognised in modern-day parents. This might be because it is being diagnosed more readily or because people are more comfortable talking about it.

Why are parents, or people in general, more anxious these days? Is it because modern parents put more pressure on themselves? Is it because they were professional people before they were parents? Is it because of social media and the social pressures associated with parenting? Is it because parents these days are less likely to live close to their parents or know their neighbours? Is it because the cost of living is higher and therefore financial strain is more prevalent?

All of the above.

As with PND, you will probably need professional support to get through persistent postnatal anxiety.

Social media

Social media is certainly not helping the postnatal mental health in modern day parents. Seeing the perfectly portrayed parenting lives of others is unhelpful and contributes to anxiety. Following mummy bloggers may or may not be useful for your mental health and expectations of parenthood. Have a think about what kind of social media you expose yourself to in the parenting department.

Sleep deprivation

Sleep deprivation is extremely depressing or anxiety producing. I found I was more and more anxious as the night time approached, knowing how long the night might be or how much sleep I wouldn't be getting. I felt so lonely through the night. Although I had a supportive partner, he needed to sleep to be safe at work. I tried not to call on him in the middle of the night. I had to find a strategy to calm myself down in the evening so I could have a little nap before Luke went to bed. Although I find it difficult to turn my busy brain off, I had some success using a mindfulness app called 'Mind the Bump': **www.mindthebump.org.au**

Loss of control

Loss of control is also contributing to anxiety in parents these days. Our generation struggles to 'go with the flow' or 'be in the moment'.

Many parents start their parenting journey on the back of a successful and rewarding career that they had control over; they could plan their day down to the minute and execute it without interruption. This won't help you be a parent.

Babies are unpredictable, things will change from day to day and you have to accept you can't control them. You'll need to take every minute, hour and day at time. Go with the flow and take it as it comes. The sooner you give in to this, the easier you will find parenting a newborn baby.

Visitors in the first weeks

This can be chaotic! You might need to put some boundaries in place until the novelty of your new baby wears off and people stop wanting to come over. Before you have the baby, have a candid chat with your loved ones about your expectations at this time. Are you happy for everyone to come and see you at the hospital? I wasn't. I was only there for two nights, I knew I'd be wrecked and I wanted to learn to breastfeed my baby. Only family and a select few friends in the hospital for me. Ask the bulk of your extended social group to give you a few weeks to settle in.

Many hospitals have quite strict visiting hours; this is to protect the time for you and your baby to bond and learn in the first few days. Some people I know like to get all the visitors out of the way in the hospital while these strict visiting hours are in place. Other hospitals have more flexible hours, but have a think about if you want a constant stream of people in and out of your room when you are physically and emotionally vulnerable.

When I was in hospital, I had no control over my bowel and bladder, I had a catheter in, I was passing wind with every wriggle in the bed. Who would you feel comfortable sharing that part of yourself with?

You also shouldn't have to time your baby's feeds around when the visitors are coming. And who are you comfortable feeding in front of?

Once we got home, my body had a lot of healing to do. If I was upright out of bed for longer than an hour, my stitches swelled up like nothing else and it was painful. If we had more than one lot of visitors per day, I didn't spend enough time in bed. I was sitting up, getting cups of tea, I didn't get my daily salt bath or I'd miss out on a much needed nap. So, my rules: family could visit whenever but only if they accepted that I might go off to sleep while they were visiting. Friends I asked to come in groups; otherwise, it would have been weeks and weeks of daily visitors.

Don't clean the house when people are visiting; no one cares. Don't bake. If they want a cup of tea, leave everything out on the bench so they can make it themselves. Get people to bring *you* food and make *you* a cup of tea!

Adjusting to parenthood

Possibly the most overwhelming part of parenting, especially with your first baby, is just getting used to the fact that your life is changed forever, you are entirely responsible for another life and you can no longer just get up and go at the drop of a hat. You can gear yourself up for this as much as you can in the pregnancy but you can't actually get your head around it until the baby is here. It can be a steep learning curve for a lot of people. I knew exactly what was coming my way but getting used to doing it day by day took a long time for me. I felt totally smothered by my baby in the first few months.

Bonding

It is normal to take ages to come to terms with the fact you are parenting a child, let alone to bond deeply with them. People talk about this instantaneous feeling of love and adoration for their baby the minute they exit the birth canal. It's not how it goes for everyone, particularly if you've had a difficult birth. Don't put that pressure on yourself when the baby first arrives. It's a waste of energy.

When Eliza was born, I did what I had to do for her out of necessity. My actions were driven by my knowledge of what my baby needed from me, not by my love for her. Over time, as my hormonal fog lifted and my baby started to offer up a few smiles, I grew to love her. Now I care for her out of practical need *and* love for her.

It takes time for some. If it doesn't grow over time, it is probably worth seeking out some further support. There are plenty of facilitated groups out there for parents who feel this way. Ask your nurse or have a look online.

Feeling overwhelmed

It is okay to feel overwhelmed. Parenting is the biggest job you'll ever have to do. There is so much unknown. You can look after other people's babies all you like but it doesn't prepare you for the relentlessness of the job you are about to undertake. Don't beat yourself up if you feel overwhelmed.

Day by day, you will grow more confident in how to do the everyday stuff like feed, change, burp and cuddle. Over time, you will learn your values as a parent and your baby's personality and that will mould how you choose to raise your child. After a few months, you'll be used to having your own baby and being a parent. There will be ups and downs but it won't be as overwhelming. Stressful at times, but not as overwhelming as having your first newborn baby. This too shall pass!

Having a lifeline

It is probably worth having a think about who might be your lifeline in the times you feel totally overwhelmed and your partner is at work. You might have a couple of people you can call on. You could make a plan to have someone drop in for an hour or so each day your partner is at work to begin with until you feel either comfortable on your own or to get out of the house on your own. At the very least, have a think about what you might do if you are alone with your baby and feeling totally overwhelmed, for example, putting your baby in their cot where they will be safe while you go and call someone.

Getting on with your life after the birth of baby

Don't try to do too much too soon. I can remember signing up for a mums and bubs exercise class at three months postpartum, thinking it was time to get back into some exercise and get my pre-baby body back.

The class was at nine am; needless to say, with a twelve-week-old baby who was still up and unsettled much of the night, I never got there. I was being too ambitious and getting ahead of myself. Give yourself some time to get used to the baby and being a parent. The cooking, cleaning and extra-curricular activities will fall back into place in time.

The modern-day parent

When it comes to parenting, there aren't going to be many quick fixes to your problems, which I think, as a millennial, is a difficult adjustment. We have become accustomed to getting solutions to problems rather rapidly, not having to wait a long time or being too patient about things. Learning to wait for a phase to pass, being patient with your unsettled baby, working hard at implementing a new routine, might be a bigger adjustment for us than the previous generations.

Another factor of being a Gen Y is that we are also the 'Google' generation. Having access to a wealth of knowledge at a drop of a hat can be useful, but can take away your trust in your own knowledge of your child and the ability to trust your instincts. We might have to work a little harder to tune into these. After a few weeks, you will know your baby better than anyone else and you will have the best idea about what is going on with them. Sure, you'll have your moments where you literally have no ***ing idea why your baby is crying. But most of the time, stop and listen to what your own instinct is telling you they want or need, and you will probably be spot on. I see it, day in and day out, a baby fussing or crying and a parent telling me, 'That's how they cry when they're hungry or tired'. Absolute gold in my eyes!

Thinking about your relationships after baby comes along

Be prepared to be impressed, shocked and everything in between when it comes to the changes your relationships might go through after this little person takes over your life.

Previously, you probably had plenty of time to focus on your relationships, giving your friend your undivided attention on the phone for an hour or a coffee date at the drop of a hat. You might have had time for a family dinner with each side of your family. You might have had a weekly date night with your partner. Your loved ones will have come to expect a certain level of presence from you – which will change.

Hopefully, your people understand the demands a baby will make on your time and accept this change. Some will think about the change only in the way that it affects them. Some might feel they have ownership over your child and that they should have unlimited access to them. It is a massive change not only for you and your partner but your whole extended family and social circle.

You might also have expectations of these people and the role they will play in supporting you. For example, you might expect your partner to stay home with you for a period of time after the baby is born. You might expect your mum to do some cooking for you or help your around the house when she visits. You might expect your friends to inquire about your baby's wellbeing frequently after the birth.

In this transitional time, most people will find themselves

shocked or disappointed by the actions of some of the people in their circle while finding others who surprise them with their level of care and attention. It is inevitable.

If it's your first baby, it is impossible to predict how you and your village will adjust their lives around this new little person. As much as you can, try to prepare for this in order to eliminate some of the drama that might overshadow your transition to parenthood. Make a clear plan with your main support person about what their presence will be after the baby is born so you both know what to expect from each other. Ask your mum, your aunt or your bestie how much they think they might be around to help – do they plan to help you in a practical sense or just come over to chat and cuddle the baby? Give them an idea about what you think might be useful for you.

Your relationship with your partner

I remember when Luke and I were getting ready for our wedding. We did something called 'pre-marriage counselling'. Pre-parenting counselling – why doesn't this exist?

At least, sit down and open up the conversation about how you expect your house to run after the baby arrives. Who will be doing the housework, the shopping, walking the dog, getting up to the baby through the night? Having a new baby is overwhelming and emotional enough without having domestic disputes or frustrations on top of it. For example, is it still acceptable for your partner to take a leisurely hour or two at the gym after his full working day? For me, that was a big fat *no*!

Having your first baby can be a difficult time for your intimate relationship.

Having previously (presumably) put each other first, you are both quickly shuffled down a rung on the ladder in favour of this new little dependant. Relationships can get a bit lost at this time, particularly if the way you communicate your love for each other is spending quality time talking, going out, making love etc. Some of the habitual activities you are used to doing together will go out the window for a while. Later, you will find new ones that accommodate the baby as well.

The best you can do is try to prepare yourselves by talking candidly about how you expect your relationship to function when the baby arrives and then be kind to each other while it falls into place. Bring up the issues that need addressing as they come along as calmly and non-accusingly as possible.

Transition to parenting for your partner

I think, in a lot of ways, becoming a parent is a trickier adjustment for your partner. They are often less comfortable handling the baby and, if you are breastfeeding, they might feel a little helpless at times. They haven't gone through the hormonal component of having a baby: the bonding might take a bit longer.

From my experience as a person who already knew how to handle a baby, I felt that it was important to give Luke a bit of space with Eliza to fumble and learn how he liked to do things without me hovering or correcting him.

It is in your best interests for your support people to feel comfortable dealing with the baby; otherwise, the baby's care will all end up on you. This can be an exhausting position to be in.

Family violence

You might be wondering why such a topic is in parenting book. Unfortunately, one in *four* women in Australia have been impacted at some stage in their life by family violence. More than one woman a week is killed by her spouse!

The incidence of family violence increases when women are pregnant and new babies are born.

If a baby lives in home where violence is occurring, it will impact negatively on all aspects of their health and wellbeing, even if they aren't witness to the violence.

What surprises most people is that family violence is not only defined as physical violence, but also emotional abuse (such as incessantly putting someone down), social (such as not allowing a family member to interact with people in their social circle), financial abuse (such as not giving someone access to their own money) and cultural (such as not letting someone participate in their own cultural practices or beliefs).

What I want to say about this is, *none* of the above is okay. The victim of family violence doesn't deserve it. There is no valid excuse for being a perpetrator of family violence.

Our biggest hurdle to overcome in relation to family violence in Australia is gender equality. Until all generations, cultures and social groups view men and women as equal, women will continue to be at a much higher risk of being a victim of violence.

What I hope to get out of mentioning this topic is that you will recognise what kind of behaviour between family members is not acceptable. I would like you to think about gender equality in your own home and how you and your partner might model this in a healthy way to your children.

Please search YouTube for attitudes to gender equality and violence against women and watch this video: **https://www.youtube.com/watch?v=8E7RGjk69T4**

Most of all, I would like you to know that if family violence is a problem for you in your house, there is a lot of help out there when you are ready to access it. If you don't feel comfortable talking to friends or family about it, please call the number or visit the website below. It is completely confidential and you can start to make changes when you feel ready.

Your child's wellbeing is probably the best reason you will ever have to make a change.

1800 RESPECT

https://www.1800respect.org.au

Ask who your local family violence service is.

Friendships

You expect that your friends will understand that you are no longer as available and you can't do all of the same activities you used to do with them.

If your friend hasn't had kids yet or has no one around them with kids, they might not get it. They might feel disappointed in you for your lack of effort and presence. There's not much you can do about this. Hopefully your friendship can hang in there until they have kids or nieces and nephews and come to understand.

It is much easier not to be the first couple in your social circle to have kids, as your friends with kids will probably have already shifted their lifestyles to suit their children. You'll probably find yourself more drawn to these friendships as they will be more relatable to you. Most people who don't have kids find it hard to talk about nappies, breastfeeding and sleepless nights.

Some friends will surprise you, stepping up and offering their support and coming to you in lieu of your usual lunch date. Some won't even ask you how your baby is or want to see your baby; those are the friendships that will disappoint you and are more likely to drift away. It is what it is. Not all friendships are forever and you will hopefully make some wonderful new friendships through your new little person.

The village

Unfortunately in most western cultures, our sense of 'village' has been lost. When I was growing up, we were friends with all our neighbours, we could play in the street and our grandparents didn't work so we were rarely in childcare. We spent all of our Christmases and holidays with our immediate and extended families. My husband and I grew up with our cousins.

Times have changed. We barely know our neighbours, our parents are still working when we have kids, we are more likely to have to go back to work quickly to pay our mortgage and more likely to use childcare. Mums are often parenting solo for twelve hours a day, day in day out.

My thoughts on this? Ditch the 'super-mum' mentality, reclaim the village! It is *not* solely up to you (the parents) to raise and care for your children. Recruit and invite the people in your life that you love and respect to help you. Get to know your neighbours, local shop vendors and kindergarten parents.

Offer your own assistance to others when you can.

Your village might consist of you and your partner, your parents, your brothers and sisters, your close friends, your mothers' group, your neighbours and whomever else you feel comfortable enough to be vulnerable with – in other words, the people you trust.

Allow these people to come and spend time with your family, to observe how you care for your baby, so they can replicate it. Let your baby become familiar with these people and come to love and trust them too. It'll benefit you as a person and a parent and it will benefit your child.

My husband and I still can't believe how important our sense of family has become since Eliza arrived. After the selfish years of early adulthood, focusing on careers, travel and partying, we have really come back to our roots and to the people who will truly love and care for Eliza throughout her lifetime.

Generational conflict and parenting advice

This is a pretty Gen Y thing to be talking about but it is a valid issue. I have had hundreds of clients have massive problems with their parents and in-laws over differing opinions on how to parent this baby.

It's a tricky one. Yes, grandparents are parents in their own right, but they parented a young baby a long time ago, in a different era. Yes, babies are still the same, but parenting isn't. The social and financial pressures are different. Thirty years ago, your family could probably survive on one wage. These days, with house and living prices through the roof, there's a good chance you both need to be back at work within a year. Furthermore, our knowledge is different. Thirty years ago, health professionals were the only experts. Today, you are capable of finding the knowledge of an expert online with the click of a button.

How to cope with it?

Remember, if the comments are coming from a loved one, they are emotionally invested in you and your child and are probably coming from the most well intentioned, loving place. Try not to get too defensive. If someone is trying to make you do something that is completely off track, give them a link to the relevant website or take them along to one of your health check-ups, mention the idea with curiosity to the health professional and let them do the talking.

You could also smile and nod and make comments like 'That's an interesting idea, I'll look into it later'. Don't completely disregard their ideas; even though their experiences were different, they probably have some pearls of wisdom that might help you.

Parent shaming

The judgement, oh, the judgement!

Parenting is fraught with it. It feels shocking to be on the receiving end so, once you feel judged for the first time as a parent, you'll probably never judge another parent again. Your new mentality? Every parent is simply doing what they need to do to get through that day.

Some quotes from wise ones in regards to this topic:

'Since I've become a parent, I will never judge another parent again!' (My cousin).

'Just don't tell people what you are doing when it comes to your parenting choices; keep it to yourself.' (My best friend).

'The problem with your generation is that you share to much'. (My work colleague).

Your child, your choice

As my girlfriend suggested, share the bare minimum of your parenting choices with the greater masses. If you want to talk nitty gritty of the difficulties you are having with your baby, try talking to other new mummies who are more likely to be going through the same thing and will have a greater empathy for the fact that you're just doing what you need to do.

The random judger in the supermarket

People who don't know you, your baby or your life story can be quick to give you a foul look or make a comment on your child's behaviour. Don't be like a client of mine who was escorted from the supermarket by security for standing up for herself to one such person. It will probably leave you feeling worse and then you will need to travel further to get your groceries. It's lose-lose.

Learn to put your thick skin on in public. If someone makes a negative comment, pretend you didn't hear them or tell them their comments are not really helping your situation and walk away.

If you see someone doing this to another parent, go and stand with them in solidarity.

If someone tries to shame you for breastfeeding your child in public, threaten to call the police – it's illegal.

Social Support

New parent group – or something like it

If you are the type of person who is already beautifully connected in a family full of kids or a social circle that's already procreating, that might be the extent of your search for peer support – good for you. Use those people to lean on and let you know that they have been through it and seen the light at the end of the tunnel. That they even went back for a second, third, fourth child. That you can survive being a new parent!

Some will get a shiver down their spine when they hear the term 'mothers' group'. I know it's not for everyone. But knowing someone who is going through or has been through the same parenting challenges as you is invaluable. Depending where you live and if it's your first baby or not, your local council might invite you to such a group of other first-time parents. Give it a go. You might not feel comfortable with that kind of social setting or you might not necessarily gel with any of the other parents, but that's shouldn't be the end of it.

Keep searching. There are pregnancy apps that can link you in with people due around the same time, there are birthing classes with people due at the same time, there are family and friends, there are new parent groups, there are playgroups, you might be able to find a local 'mums club' on Facebook, there are other online forums.

Keep putting yourself out there until you connect with

someone. Use whatever stops you from being isolated in this critical period of time in the life of you and your baby! Hey, there is even a new 'Tinder for mums' app out there now – I'm all for it! https://www.letsmush.com/

The important thing, I think, is that you can find at least a couple of real people who won't pretend that their life and their child is perfect and will share their everyday ups and downs as a parent with you. I can't stress enough how helpful this is for most new parents!

I was extremely lucky to have a few friends at similar stages in life with young babies around Eliza's age. I also connected with my local mothers' group through my local council – a bunch of fantastic, easy-going and *real* people, who weren't afraid to share that, yes, their child too had been the devil incarnate that week, that they were getting no sleep or that they were struggling to breastfeed. On a day when I felt so low with failure as a parent, just to have someone say, 'Oh, my child is behaving that way too at the moment' is enough to pull you off the ledge.

So I'd urge you to find your 'people' in whatever way you feel comfortable and share your struggles with them because they'll get it and there's nothing more reassuring as a new parent.

Some of my mothers' group babies

Getting out of the house

This can be so daunting to begin with. I can remember giving myself forty-five minutes to get to a baby health check appointment at an office that was five minutes from my house. It can take a lot of organisation to begin with but the more you do it, the more efficient it will become. Start small. Don't be overly ambitious. Maybe take your mum everywhere with you for the first month or so until you build up your confidence.

Most shopping centres will have a baby room where you can feed and change and there will be a toilet that your pram will fit into if you need to go. Suss out your local shopping centre before bubs arrives.

Visits to a friend's house where you feel comfortable feeding are a great start too. If you need a cup of tea or to go to the toilet, your friend can hold the baby!

Babies are notorious for cracking it in the middle of your grocery shopping, so it might be a bit ambitious to do this solo in the first couple of months. Online shopping might be a good option if your partner doesn't have time to do the shopping or buys the wrong stuff. You can then pop out with baby for short twenty-minute fresh food shops and abandon ship if the baby cracks it.

You may have trouble with your breastfeeding or giving a bit of formula here and there, like I did. I took some boiled water and some formula with me wherever I went, just in case. Nothing worse than having a screaming hungry baby who won't latch in a public place.

Take a change of clothes, a few nappies and wipes everywhere you go. Babies are great at pooing up their backs in the first few months. If you're tempted to go out anywhere without your nappy bag, I would always have a onesie, some nappies and a packet of wipes in the car.

Learn to use your pram before the baby is born. I got caught out on this one but luckily had a car big enough that I could stuff the whole pram in the boot without collapsing it. The same goes for the baby carrier – you're not going to be able to wing it. Luke and I spent about two hours watching and re-watching an instructional video on YouTube before we got the hang of our Ergo Baby!

Sleep

This is such a huge topic and one that everyone in your village will have an opinion about!

I am a big lover of a full night's sleep. But as my wise husband said to me somewhere during our first year of parenthood, 'Just let it go, Sarah! Once you are a parent, you're not supposed to get solid sleep.'

So let's start this chapter by swallowing that jagged little pill, shall we?

Reading baby sleep books

If I had a dollar for every infant sleep book I've read! The angst they can cause when parents try to follow them to the word…argh!

The baby hasn't read the book!

Having knowledge is power. So, by all means, read the book, learn about what are normal newborn sleep patterns and how often they usually sleep and eat so you have a bit of a guide. But don't expect your baby to follow a regimented routine – it's futile. You'll feel like a failure or frustrated with your baby for not following it.

Sometimes they are hungry earlier than the book says to feed them; what are you going to do? Let a hungry baby cry for an hour? How stressful!

The fourth trimester

In the first few weeks, your baby should basically feed and sleep. They will lull you into a false sense of security that they are a 'really chilled' baby; that is, good sleepers. Then, boom, they'll wake up and start clinging to you all day like a koala and screaming for hours on end in the evening.

Your baby has been in your tummy for nine months, wrapped up and contained right next to your heartbeat. This is how they would like to continue for what we call 'the fourth trimester'.

Try not to fight it too much. If they want to be cuddled, then cuddle them. If you want to have a sleep yourself, see if someone else can cuddle them. When baby seems relaxed and receptive to it, put them in their own bed for a sleep. If it doesn't work, cuddle them.

The witching hour

Around the two-week mark, most babies will start to have what we call a 'witching hour'. This means they have a period in the day when they are more unsettled, they may cluster-feed, they may seem uncomfortable with wind or cry for no reason. It might go on for a few hours.

This behaviour is actually a normal developmental phase that babies go through. Depending on the temperament of the baby, they may cry more or less than your average baby.

A lot of people would call this 'colic'. Like colic, this unsettled period peaks around six week of age and usually settles by the time they are three months old. Hang in there!

As discussed earlier, if your baby is excessively unsettled around the clock, this is not normal and it would be a good idea to discuss this behaviour with your health nurse, GP or paediatrician.

Management of the witching hour

When babies are having their witching hour, you simply need to do whatever you need to do to get through that time. Where possible, have someone else present at this time to take a turn nursing the unsettled baby. This will save your sanity and stop you from feeling frustrated with them.

Offer the baby a feed when he seems hungry, give him a bit of a burp and a cuddle and change his nappy if need be. Repeat until the baby settles.

That's it.

If the baby's unsettled period is in the evening, aim to do a bath in the late evening which will either calm him down or tucker him out. Give him one last big feed for the evening and cross your fingers for a longish (three to four hours) stretch of sleep.

Any minutes of sleep you get before midnight are a bonus at this age, so try not to stress too much about getting to bed at a reasonable hour. Babies are notoriously unsettled during those late evening hours.

Feed, burp, cuddle, change: repeat until baby settles.

Overnight

Night time should not include any play time. Of course you can't stop them from waking up, and initially they might be wakeful or unsettled after the night time feeds, but it is important to reinforce that it is night time by not turning all the lights on or engaging in active play such as tummy time or nursery rhymes. Only change the nappy if you need to.

Over time, the baby will learn that night time is for sleep and, although they will still need to feed, they should go straight back to sleep.

During the day

Equally, babies should be exposed natural light when they are wakeful in the day. This will give their body exposure to the regular twenty-four-hour circadian rhythm that most humans follow. Daily light exposure throughout the day will gear up their little bodies to know that night time is coming.

Sleep routines

In the second month of life they will become more aware of their surroundings and more aware of their (and your) sleep and settling habits. Try to recognise what they look like when they're tired – their 'tired signs': **http://raisingchildren.net.au/articles/baby_cues_tired_video.html**

Tired signs

If you are unsure of your baby's tired signs, look at the clock and time the standard amount of awake time for your baby's age (see below). You might start to see some early 'tired signs' like red eyebrows, averting your gaze or becoming a bit awkward and jerky.

Average awake time

1) Newborn babies: barely any.

2) 1 month old: maybe an hour max.

3) 3 months old: usually about 1.5 hours, 3 naps a day.

4) 6 months old: usually about 2 hours, 3 naps a day.

5) 8 months old: usually about 3 hours, 2 naps a day.

6) 12–18 months old: 4-5 hours in the morning, 1 nap middle of the day.

Sleepy-time routine

Make up a bedtime routine that you follow each time they seem tired. For example, you take them to their room, put them in their sleeping bag, close the blinds, give them a cuddle and a kiss, lay them in their bed and say goodnight and walk out of the room.

Give them some space to grizzle and grumble. If they become distressed and cry continuously for more than 30 seconds, try to give them a reassuring pat and 'shhh' while they lie in their cot. If this doesn't work, pick them up and cuddle them. Try again next time.

Sleep cycles

'Sleep cycle' is the term we use to describe the process of falling asleep, going into a deep sleep and coming back to a light sleep.

If you think about your own night's sleep, you don't close your eyes and stay in the same position all night. You roll over, rouse a little, get up to the toilet and go back to sleep. Don't expect your babies to lie there quietly either. In fact, babies are even noisier, their sleep cycles are much shorter than ours (around twenty to forty-five minutes) and they will rouse more often.

If your baby only sleeps around thirty minutes then wakes, she has had what we call a 'catnap', one sleep cycle. This isn't enough for most babies to be restored and they will generally be grisly or feed poorly after a catnap. If this is your baby, try to observe them starting to rouse and give them a pat or a cuddle through their lighter sleep phase to get them down into another sleep cycle.

As they get older, if they learn to fall asleep in their bed independently, they should learn to rouse from one sleep cycle, recognise their sleep environment and go back down for another sleep cycle.

Saying this, as they get older, some babies naturally develop into 'catnappers'. They sleep thirty minutes, they're up and they're happy. They eat and play well; nothing to be fixed there. Certainly not so easy for those parents who try to fit a meal and a shower in that time.

We'll discuss individual sleep patterns later.

Feed, play, sleep

This is a very loose kind of routine for people to follow, one that doesn't dictate feed times or sleep times.

Basically, when your baby wakes from a nap, feed them, have some play time and watch for your baby's tired signs.

Once you notice your baby's tired signs, say to baby, 'You're tired! Let's go to bed.' Take them to their sleep space, which should be dark and quietish (background household noise is totally fine), and follow your sleepy time routine.

That's it. When they wake, repeat.

Obviously every day will be different, and sometimes it won't work, but it's a guide for those who like to have something to follow.

This is the foundation. If you know this foundation information from the get-go, when the time is right, you will learn what your baby's tired signs are, you will make a predictable bedtime routine and environment for them and they will start to recognise and respond to it.

Night waking and feeding in the second half of the year

The majority of babies will continue to feed in the night past six months, particularly breastfed babies. If you're lucky, they'll drop it earlier, but it's good to have realistic expectations about this so you don't feel disappointed or cheated when they don't.

If someone tells you their two-month-old baby sleeps through the night, don't despair. Their concept of 'sleeping through' might be one stretch of five hours' sleep.

The dream feed

Once their baby can sleep for a really good stretch of time, say six to eight hours, many parents will try a 'dream feed'. This means putting your baby down for bed of a night, say, eight pm, and getting them up for a feed before you go bed yourself at around ten or eleven pm. The hope is, once you give the dream feed, that bubs could sleep through until the morning. It doesn't work for everyone. I personally put Eliza down for the night and let her wake up in the middle of the night when she was ready for a feed. Whatever works.

Sleeping through the night

Once they are sleeping through, that's it, right? Full night sleeps forever!

Unfortunately, no. Babies will wake through the night, even once they don't need a feed, for a variety of reasons. Teething is a big one, which we'll discuss in another chapter. Illness is another, as are developmental phases, or 'wonder weeks', and separation anxiety.

You might have heard of 'sleep regressions'. While this can be a real thing for lots of kids, I don't think it's worth you having a certain time or age in your mind; for example, a sleep regression that is expected around four months.

As with everything else, kids are individual. Eliza rarely did things 'on time'. Yes, she had times when her sleep was worse than usual, but what's the point in getting all worked up with anticipation for something that may or may not happen? The anticipation will hurt you more than the actual event. And then, it might not happen at all – bonus!

Management of night waking

As long as you have a baby who is in the swing of self-settling in their own sleep space, as we've discussed earlier, you really just need to ride out any sleep regressions.

If they are teething or unwell, they might be uncomfortable. Give them some analgesia.

If they have been eating poorly because of illness or teething, they might be hungry. Feed them.

If they are going through an intense period of separation anxiety, they might need a cuddle and for you to sit with them while they resettle.

Yes I know: don't get into bad habits! But if it's just a phase, do what you need to do for everyone to get through it comfortably. Don't be too hard on yourself or your baby.

> *Your baby doesn't stop needing you because its night time.*
>
> *This too shall pass.*
>
> *If it doesn't, have a chat to your peers or your health nurse.*

Crappy sleepers

Some babies are crappy sleepers. No matter how well you lay down the foundations as above, they will challenge you and you will do whatever you need to do to get some 'shut eye'. One way or another, they won't still be getting up and wanting to breastfeed or cuddle in bed when they're eighteen.

Chant yourself the parenting mantra: 'this too shall pass' and have a chat to someone who can go through the whole situation with you from an outsider's point of view. They might be able to identify some things in your routine that you can change. Work on it and if you're becoming insane, look into going to sleep school or calling in a private sleep consultant who can give you some hands-on support to train them to sleep a bit more independently.

Individual sleep patterns

The real issue I have with most baby sleep books is that they don't take into account that individual babies have individual sleep needs. Just like adults, they don't all sleep for the same amount of time each day and night. Hence, following a rigid time schedule is difficult. So get to know *your* baby and their needs.

I've had clients whose babies don't sleep at all in the day but they'll sleep all night; babies who only catnap but wake up happy and ready to start their day again after only thirty minutes sleep; babies or toddlers who literally only need nine hours of sleep at night like some adults and they are eating and developing well, happy and growing.

What's the point of trying to fight what's most likely pre-programed inside them? Go with it. Everyone will be happier.

Sleep is not always perfect. You can do your best to implement these strategies but don't let it ruin your day if things don't go exactly to plan. Some days you will be out and about and your baby will need to have short sleeps in the car or pram. Sometimes they won't sleep when you expect them to. Sometimes it'll be Christmas, a birthday or Mother's Day.

Have a consistent sleep and bedtime routine if it suits you and be flexible enough to let it go on the days it doesn't or the baby isn't going for it.

SIDS

Sudden Infant Death Syndrome is a devastating circumstance where an infant dies in their sleep with no obvious cause. It could be related to asphyxiation. What we know about SIDS is that there are things we can do to reduce the risk, most importantly that the baby is sleeping in a safe environment.

This means:

1) they sleep on their back
2) they have their own sleep space (not shared with a parent)
3) their mattress is firm and fits the cot snuggly
4) they don't have any soft bedding around them that they could potentially smother themselves with
5) they have plenty of air flow
6) they are not exposed to cigarette smoke.

Babies are much more likely to die of SIDS if they sleep in the same bed as a parent who has been drinking, smoking or doing drugs, as are babies who are put to sleep on couches or bean bags.

The newest SIDS 'safe sleeping' recommendation is to have the baby in the same room as you. Research shows that when you share a room, it makes you more attune to the baby's needs and therefore you attend to them more frequently in the night.

I personally found it very difficult to sleep with Eliza in my room. She was a grumbly, grunty little baby and I found it hard to go off to sleep while listening to her. Given that sleep was so precious to me in the early months, I opted to have Eliza in her own room from an early age so that I couldn't hear all the little grizzles and grumbles, but could hear the legitimate crying that needed attention. I certainly didn't follow that part of the SIDS guidelines but I desperately needed to sleep. See what feels right for you.

Apnoea monitors

I have had the occasional parent who is so nervous about SIDS that they use an apnoea monitor on their baby, which would alert you if they stopped breathing. The equipment is a little expensive but if it gives you peace of mind and a bit more rest, I'm all for it.

A word about co-sleeping

Co-sleeping is a very taboo topic. I'm not going to put my hand up and directly tell you to do it but the reality of the matter is that many families do it at some point in time. For many countries and cultures, it is the norm. I certainly slept with Eliza for the first couple of weeks because it felt like the right thing to do and I was struggling to sit up to feed.

I believe we should be more upfront about it and talk about the safest way to do it if that's what people are secretly doing anyway. In an ideal world, babies sleep in their own sleep space. By the same token, we know that breastfeeding is one of the most protective things you can do against SIDS and that co-sleeping promotes breastfeeding.

Some people are just trying to survive by getting half an

hour of sleep and they can't seem to manage it through the night with no one else to hold their unsettled baby.

So, if you need or choose to do it:

1) your mattress must be firm enough that if your baby rolled over, they wouldn't get smothered.

2) you must not be taking drugs, drinking or smoking.

3) the baby mustn't be near any soft bedding that might cover their face.

4) ideally, kick your partner out of the bed so you've got a bit more space to do this comfortably.

Have a read of the Red Nose articles here: **https://rednose.com.au/article/sharing-a-sleep-surface-with-a-baby**

A note about swaddling

Once your baby starts to roll, it's time to stop swaddling them. They need their arms to push themselves off their face and even roll themselves back over.

Time to transition to a sleeping bag with arms out.

Some babies are a little unsettled by the newfound freedom in their arms. You can do one arm at a time, but it doesn't take them long to get used to it!

I rolled the mittens on Eliza's onesies over her hands for the first week or two while she learnt to have her arms flapping around before I gave her hands as well.

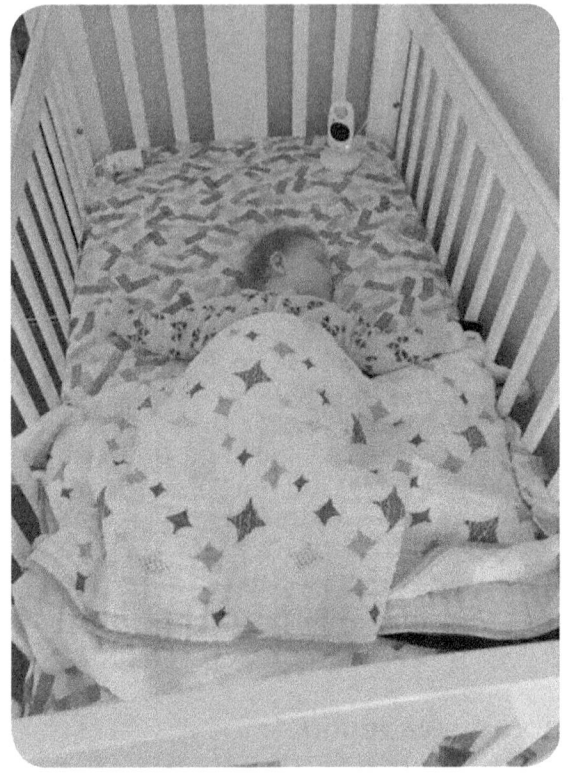

I didn't have to transition Eliza out of her swaddle until about nine months as she took so long to learn to roll!

Choosing your GP and meeting your health nurse

Depending on the state you live in, the professional health support that is available to you and your child will differ slightly. Most states have some form of community nurse who might be a parenting worker, a Division One nurse, a midwife, a maternal health nurse or all of the above. They might offer regular health checks for the first few years or they might only weigh and measure your baby. Ask your hospital midwife who will be taking over your care when you go home.

On top of this, you should also aim to build a relationship with a regular GP practice with two or three doctors whom you feel comfortable seeing with your baby.

For some families, the support of their health nurse and GP are pivotal in their wellbeing in the early years. So it makes a lot of sense, if you don't feel well supported or connected to your health care provider, that you should probably look for someone who suits your needs a bit better. You are not obliged to continue to see the nurse or GP who has been allocated to you. If you think you could be better supported, ask to see someone else.

A great way to find a good GP is through word of mouth. Ask your friends, family and neighbours in the area who they've seen and been happy with. Find a clinic that accepts new appointments on the day for unwell children and who preferably bulk bills.

Growth

If your pregnancy is normal and healthy, your baby will generally be born the size that is genetically predisposed by you, the parents. For example, my brother and I were quite big babies, around 4 kgs. My husband on the other hand was smaller, around 3 kgs. Naturally, I crossed my fingers for a compact little 3 kgs baby, but alas, my genes came through with the goods – out came a boofer baby like me. Eliza weighed in at 3.91 kgs! All the staff at the birth thought it was hysterical that such a big baby came out of little me.

My point is, size is generally determined by genetics. We talk about children's sizes in terms of 'percentiles.' This means an average size baby for that age and sex will be around the 50th percentile, where a smaller baby will be around the 5th percentile and a bigger around the 90th percentile, where a smaller baby will be around the 5th percentile and a bigger around the 90th percentile. It absolutely doesn't matter which percentile your baby is on, as long as they grow! So whether your baby is born big or little, as long as they're fed and they grow, it's all good.

Standard growth patterns

Most babies will be born with a bit of extra fluid on board which their body will excrete in the first forty-eight hours. Therefore, most babies will lose weight in the first few days. Babies born to mums who had an IV drip in labour will generally have a bit more fluid when they're born.

It is totally acceptable for a baby to lose up to 10% of their birth weight.

Once the milk comes in, around day 3–5, and the baby is getting a larger volume with each feed, they will start to regain weight. In the first couple of weeks, this might be minimal, but as long as the baby doesn't continue to lose weight, he is weeing, his poos are moving away from that black colour and he is not too jaundiced or drowsy, it's all good.

After about the two-week mark, babies will start to gain roughly 30 grams per day. Obviously, this will vary slightly, depending on the baby, and this is where the percentile charts come in.

Our infant growth charts are provided by the World Health Organisation and the Centre for Disease Control and reflect the growth of breastfed babies across the world: http://www.education.vic.gov.au/childhood/parents/mch/Pages/charts.aspx

As your baby is weighed and measured, your health nurse will be able to plot their growth and tell you where your baby sits in terms of size compared to the rest of his peers around the world and, more importantly, that he is tracking along the growth curve.

Please don't worry if your baby is not 'average'. Like I said, size is genetically predisposed. Just like adults, they are all different. If you put me on the chart now as an adult, I would be on the 5th percentile, but there's nothing wrong with me! (???) I just come from a family of short-statured people. As long as your baby follows the growth curve, you are doing great!

Deviations from the growth curve

Babies will often cross growth curves, becoming a higher or lower percentile. Your health nurse should be able to give you some advice as to why this is happening. It is not always a big concern.

If, for example, your baby drops down a percentile for weight but the height and head are growing consistently and your baby is happy and settled, there is probably no need for panic.

If your baby is soaring up on the weight percentile, this is probably not a reason for concern either, as long as you are not force-feeding your baby. Babies are supposed to be chubby. Once they crawl and walk, they start to drop some extra fat and the weight percentile will settle down again.

Immunisations

Immunisation is available to you for free in Australia and is designed to prevent your child from contracting preventable, potentially deadly diseases.

It's a big topic and most people get the sense that it is something they'd like to do for their children without having to think too deeply about it.

If you choose to immunise, you can start this after baby turns six weeks old. Your health nurse should give you more information about how to access this through either your local council or your GP.

If you want to make sure you don't forget, you can download the Vax on Time app to remind you when bubs is due: **https:// itunes.apple.com/au/app/vaxontime-immunisation- reminders-for-parents-who-live/id1063193669?mt=8**

Choosing not to vaccinate

Some families look into immunisation in great depth, do a lot of research and decide it's not for them. I respect each parent's wish to do what they feel is best for their child. I've had many clients choose not to immunise and that's their prerogative.

However, immunisation is proven through robust scientific studies to be safe and effective in preventing children from contracting the diseases. There is not, however, any solid research that tells us it is *not* safe. There is plenty of 'research' out there, but the studies aren't considered to be 'robust' in terms of the study design. You will certainly be able to find 'research' against immunisation on the internet, but unless you have a good grasp on what is reputable research, reading up online is probably a not the best way to make your decision.

I would recommend talking to someone in the immunisation department at, for example, your local council or children's hospital about your concerns. A good place to start is the Immunise Australia website: http://www.immunise.health.gov.au/

Not vaccinating your children will have implications for your ability to access childcare, kindergarten and Centrelink payments. Your child will obviously be more vulnerable to contracting those preventable diseases, particularly when you travel or if you live in an area with a high rate of non-vaccinators.

Extra self-funded vaccinations

There are a few additional vaccinations on top of the normal childhood schedule that you can choose to give as extras at your own expense. These might include a yearly flu vaccination, a course of extra meningococcal vaccines and a chicken pox booster. Ask the provider who is vaccinating your child about them.

Dr Google

Speaking of researching online, this a probably a good time to talk about using 'Dr Google'. It can do you more harm than good if you find yourself in the wrong place. There is so much garbage on the internet; anyone can write whatever they want there. Be careful to take what you read, on a blog for example, with a grain of salt and *never* take medical advice from the internet.

If you're concerned about your baby, get him checked by a professional in the flesh.

When looking online, a good way to sift out some of the crap from the reputable information is by looking at the source of the information. Any blog or website ending in '.com' is probably not regulated by any sort of government, medical or health care institution. Here's some examples of websites that are reputable, regulated and contain information that is evidence-based:

1) http://raisingchildren.net.au
2) http://www.rch.org.au/home/
3) https://www.breastfeeding.asn.au
4) http://www.panda.org.au
5) https://www.thewomens.org.au

Introducing solid food

Milk should be the main source of your baby's nutrition for most of the first year.

When it comes to solids, there is a plethora of information out there and plenty of conflicting information at that. Unfortunately this makes it feel more complicated than what it is, which causes undue stress for parents.

In Victoria, health nurses educate their families based on the 'Infant Feeding Guideline' by the National Health and Medical Research Council (NHMRC) as well as some fact sheets from the Royal Children's Hospital. You can access the links to these here: **https://www.nhmrc.gov.au/_files_nhmrc/file/publications/170131_n56_infant_feeding_guidelines_summary.pdf**

http://www.rch.org.au/uploadedfiles/main/content/nutrition/2013nutritionfirstyeardeecd.pdf

http://www.rch.org.au/uploadedFiles/Main/Content/nutrition/resources/Nestle%20Baby%27s%20foods%201st%20year%202014.pdf

As a maternal health nurse, I put pressure on myself to follow the Guideline as closely as possible, knowing full well what my child should be having in her diet. While it is a rather loosely worded document which accommodates for a variety of different approaches to introducing solids, I still felt like a bit of a failure when my child was very late to start to manage lumpy food and finger food. Also, she loved her milk and continues to have a bottle well after her first birthday, which goes against what the guideline suggests.

The Infant Feeding Guideline is a great source of information that provides a very flexible approach to introducing solids. However, keep in mind that it's only a guide. As long as you are working towards an end goal, which is a balanced diet of healthy family foods from all of the five food groups, it doesn't really matter how you get there.

Signs of readiness

Between four and six months, your baby will likely start to show some signs they are ready to try some food. They should have developed neck control and be showing some interest in you and your family when you eat. When you try to give them some food, they should no longer have their 'tongue protrusion reflex' that inhibits their ability to take food in their mouth and swallow it. If you offer them some food on a spoon and they spit it all out, they probably still have the reflex; try again in a few weeks.

If they are showing you all the signs on the outside that they are ready to eat, their digestive system is probably ready to digest.

Current evidence tells us that no baby's digestive system is ready any earlier than four months.

Texture and amount

Most people will have the most success starting with smoothly textured foods, such as pureed fruit or vegetables. It's not to say you can't start with a pork chop if that's your wish. You've probably heard of 'baby-led weaning' (basically only giving your baby finger food with no spoon feeding), which is all good and well. But in all honesty, for those babies who are at the slower end of their fine motor development, they are going to fall behind in the 'getting the food in the mouth and swallowing it' department.

I think spoon-feeding, while offering a bit of finger food for baby to handle with each meal, is a good way to start. You know they are actually getting to eat a few things while exploring and practising with a whole lot of foods too.

You can go straight to a mashed texture if your baby is happy with it. In my experience, lots if families say their baby isn't happy with lumpy to begin with, so puree is fine. You can work up to mashed texture, followed by small pieces and, finally, family foods. There's plenty of time to get there.

> *Babies don't need teeth to chew. They don't get their first molars until after their birthday. They will be able to tolerate all foods that are soft enough to munch with their gums.*

Gagging

Some babies will gag when they first try solid food and as they progress through the different textures. This is really normal and not a choking hazard. Their gag reflex is much more sensitive than ours and gagging will pass as they master each phase of textured food from smooth to full family foods.

Frequency

Start with once a day. In the early months, food is still for learning and you don't want it to reduce their milk volumes. If they've already had their milk, they can decide how much of the food they want to eat. Once they are into it and taking a couple of tablespoons in one go, you can add in a second meal and so on.

Milk/food ratio

Milk should remain their source of nutrition for the most part of the first year while working towards them having a balanced diet of family foods from their first birthday onwards. As they build up their food volumes and work towards having three meals a day, they will naturally drop off their milk intake.

This should happen pretty naturally but you might start to think about which milk feeds you drop in the daytime hours in lieu of a food meal around eight or nine months. Most people will keep going with at least morning and evening milk until the baby's birthday, after which time it's up to you whether they continue to breastfeed or have any bottles at all. If they had three serves of dairy in the day, you could ditch the breastfeeding and bottles all together.

The Raising Children Network is a wonderful parenting resource and has a good page on the 'serving sizes' required to get a balance of all the food groups after their first birthday: **http://raisingchildren.net.au/articles/dietary_guidelines_1-2_years_pip.html/context/225**

What foods to give

What foods should you give? This is where the mixed messages get really messy out there. As per the NHMRC current guidelines, the only foods they can't have in the first year are raw egg and honey. That's it.

There are a few other definite instructions in the Guideline.

Relatively new research tells us that introducing high allergen foods in the first few months of the eating journey in conjunction with breastfeeding will actually protect your child or reduce the risk of developing food allergy.

They also recommend early intake of foods high in iron due to depleting iron stores in breastfed babies around six months of age.

Your baby's fish intake should reflect what was recommended in your pregnancy to avoid unsafe levels of mercury in their system.

In terms of strict 'rules', that's about it.

One new food at a time?

Clients tell me they are trying each new food for three days before introducing another. Logistically, wouldn't it take something like sixty years to try all new foods if we did that?

So within reason, you can start offering a variety of new foods together on a day-to-day basis, for example, a blend of different veggies or fruits.

The foods that induce allergy responses at a higher rate are eggs, nut products, fish and shellfish, wheat and dairy. Perhaps a happy medium is to try these foods singularly, so that if they do induce an allergy response, you know exactly what has caused it.

The Australian Society of Clinical Immunology and Allergy (ASCIA) has a good guideline on this topic for families introducing high allergen foods to their babies: **https://www.allergy.org.au/patients/allergy-prevention/ascia-guidelines-for-infant-feeding-and-allergy-prevention**

Preparing baby food

I'm not going to go into excessive detail about how to prepare baby food, what to cook etc. If you need some inspiration on what to cook for bubs, have a look online or buy a baby cookbook.

If you have a pretty well rounded diet in your household, you should be able to look at what you're eating and make some adaptations so bubs can just eat a bit of what you're having. For example, if you cook a roast for the family, mash up some of the potato and pumpkin – voilà, baby food! You're having a banana for morning tea? Break a piece off, mash – voilà, more baby food! Get the gist?

Most people will do a bit of a cook-up once or twice a week in the early months, steaming hard fruits and veggies, blending them into a variety of combos and putting them in little baby ice cube containers. When the baby is having such small amounts in the beginning, defrosting one or two cubes at a time is super-simple. In that way, you can use these cubes when your family meals that day are not adaptable to baby food.

When your baby can tolerate a bit of texture (which might be from the get-go or might not be until one year old (like Eliza), you can blend or mash up meat, veggie and grain combos.

Once your baby has the dexterity to grasp food and put it in his mouth, you can start giving him finger food such as bits of toast, soft fruit, cooked vegetables and meat, crackers etc

Most kids can't spoon feed themselves until well after their first birthday so a combination of you feeding them with the spoon and them feeding themselves finger food is a winner, I'd say.

On Mum's menu: smashed avocado and eggs on crispbread, on Eliza's menu: smashed avocado

Kids take to solids at different rates and that is absolutely fine. They all get there in the end.

For babies to develop a happy and healthy relationship with food, it is important for them to sit down with the family and observe everyone else eating.

It is also important that you don't force feed them - they'll start to find mealtimes unpleasant. Don't force it if they refuse; let them see you eat it yourself or try again later.

'You're saying I'm supposed to eat this?!'

How to wean breastfeeding

This might happen naturally for many babies as they increase their solid meals in the second half of the year. They will gradually reduce the amount of breast milk they take from you, which will naturally reduce the amount of milk you produce.

If you would like to stop or reduce the amount you breastfeed before this time, you will have to actively reduce the amount you feed the baby to slowly reduce your supply. If you do this before your baby turns one, you will need to replace the breastfeeds with bottles of formula.

In order to reduce your milk supply, simply remove less milk from your breasts; that is, feed the baby for a shorter amount of time or less often.

An example of how you might do this is, drop one breastfeed every few days, replacing those feeds with bottles until the baby is fully formula-fed and your breasts feel comfortable to be left alone without any feeding or pumping.

Breastfeeding beyond the first year

The World Health Organisation recommends exclusive breastfeeding for six months, then in conjunction with solid foods up until two years of age and beyond.

Your child can get his full quota of nutrients from a balanced family diet after the first year, but there are still dietary and health benefits to continuing breastfeeding beyond that time, should you and your babe choose it.

Bottle-feeding beyond the first year

Bottle-fed babies can transition to full cream cow's milk in a cup after their birthday. Eliza continues to *love* her bottle before bed. While it is not necessary from a nutritional point of view and is considered to be a risk for her dental health, it is a part of our nightly routine and it works for us. I clean her teeth twice a day and watch them closely. She still has a dummy too. It's not the end of the world.

Water and sippy cups

Once your baby is eating food on a daily basis, they will need to learn to drink a bit of water with it. Most parents will offer water in a sippy cup. Sippy cups are pretty hit-and-miss. It takes a lot of babies a while to get the hang of it and you'll probably buy different types of cups – open cup, baby spout, sippy straw, bottle – before you have some success. Not all babies take to water straight away, but keep offering.

Eliza liked the look of her dad drinking out of his pump bottle after his gym workout and naturally wanted to try sipping it herself. We bought her own little pump bottle until she got the hang of a cup. Many will offer water in a baby bottle because they are familiar to the baby.

In the beginning, they'll still be getting heaps of water in their milk but later in the year as the solid food increases and the milk drops, they'll need the extra fluid to be well hydrated and to stop them from getting constipated.

Changing stool patterns and constipation after starting solids

Many babies' little digestive systems take a while to adjust to digesting solid foods and they may have a bit of constipation in this time. Constipation can be extremely distressing for all involved and is better avoided in the first place. So, how do we avoid it?

Firstly, offer water with foods.

Secondly, don't feed your baby an excessive amount of iron-fortified cereals. The iron in large amounts can be constipating.

Offer foods that are rich in fibre but don't load them up with fibrous foods without adding water to the equation. If they don't have fluid with it, the fibre binds them up more!

If you follow all of the above and your baby is still having hard poos, you might need to have a chat to your health care provider or pharmacist. I had to give Eliza a stool softener for a short period of time in the first few months of her eating solid food until her digestive system adjusted and she learnt to drink a bit more water.

Poo will obviously be a bit more 'solid' once babies are eating solid food, but it shouldn't be hard and it shouldn't be hard for them to push out.

Supermarket food

There is almost half an aisle dedicated in every supermarket to pre-made baby foods. They are so prominent these days that most people will naturally feel that commercial baby food is a standard thing to include in a baby's diet. In reality, they are really just convenience foods for babies.

It is worth questioning the ingredient list in anything you buy in the baby aisle. I got tricked by a few things in this department.

Many of the commercial baby foods will have a lot of sweet fruit like apple to make it taste nice, even the veggies! Do you want to teach your baby that all foods taste nice and sweet like apples or do you want to have a look at which ones you can buy with just veggies? Worth thinking about.

The texture of commercial baby food is extremely smooth as a result of the efficient factory equipment they use to blend the food. If babies get used to this texture, it can be difficult to transition between home-made and supermarket food.

The chunkier commercial baby meals such as pasta bolognese will be made with meat, veggies, pasta and 'reconstituted tomato paste'. Reconstituted tomato paste is highly processed and extremely sweet.

Some baby yoghurt may as well be in the 'sometimes' food group with the amount of sugar they have in them.

If you plan on buying supermarket food as part of your baby's diet (which I did – don't get me wrong, the convenience is amazing!), you must take the time to see what is really in it, particularly sugar content. Make an informed decision about how much you want to use them.

While your baby is eating in very small volumes, you might use a quarter of a pouch of baby food at a time. You should be able to put the rest in the fridge for a few days. If you made the same thing at home, you would make a big batch and freeze it in ice cube trays, defrosting a few at a time. Cost-wise, it's probably comparable. Home-cooked will obviously take more time.

Sugar

Sugar intake is a major cause of disease in Australia. There is added salt or sugar in almost all of our processed packaged foods. Australia has the highest level of obesity in children, which is horrifying! If you're interested in this topic, there is a fantastic documentary called 'Fed Up' which is set in the USA but still completely relevant to us. It is both terrifying and informative: http://fedupmovie.com/

I'm a big fan of sweets so naturally Eliza will be exposed to them at home and on special occasions; I have no problem with that. But, for a child's long-term health, it is important for refined sugar and processed commercial products to not be part of their daily diets.

Family food with herbs, spices and salt

As soon as you can give your baby some adaptation of what your family is eating, go for it. It will be easier for you and you want them to learn about the food you eat in your household.

Herbs and spices are totally fine; obviously, babies won't cope with super-spicy things to begin with.

Babies don't need and shouldn't have added salt to their food, so if you use a lot of it, take a portion of food out for bubs before you add it.

Foods that babies don't need

Babies don't need juice or any other sweet drinks. Water and milk – that's it! People think juice is healthy because it's fruit but, if you really think about it, children only need two or three serves of fruit a day, yet they will often get this whole amount in just one glass of juice. On top of this, the fibre that comes from eating the whole piece of fruit is usually reduced in a glass of juice. Therefore the sugar in the fruit juice is not metabolised in the same efficient way it is when that fibre is also present.

Sweet cakes, biscuits, lollies, chocolate – these shouldn't become part of a daily diet. They have no nutritional content. Over time, children will come to know those foods are in the house and refuse to eat their healthy food because of them.

Food allergies

Food reactions can come in a variety of presentations and severities. The mildest reaction is a bit of a rash around the mouth. It's important to take note of a rash if you see one. You'll need to seek medical advice about how to proceed with exposing your baby to more of that food. Most kids who get a mild rash when consuming a food will grow out of this kind allergy over time.

A more extreme reaction would include swelling of the mouth and tongue, potentially wheezing and difficulty breathing. This is an extremely serious reaction called anaphylaxis. If your baby consumes a food and is having trouble breathing, call an ambulance! Children with anaphylactic allergies need to have an adrenalin 'Epipen' with them at all times. Luckily, anaphylaxis is not super-common.

Foods that more commonly cause these kind of allergies are dairy products, eggs, peanuts, soy products, tree nuts (such as walnuts and cashews), fish and shellfish (such as prawns).

For more information: http://www.rch.org.au/kidsinfo/fact_sheets/Allergic_and_anaphylactic_reactions/

A different type of reaction is that of profuse vomiting after ingesting a food. This kind of reaction is not regulated by the immune system, but rather the gastrointestinal system. If your baby vomits profusely, they are at risk of dehydration and could possibly require hospitalisation. The most common causes of this kind of reaction are rice, cow's milk (dairy) and soy.

If you are concerned your baby has had a reaction to a food, get some medical guidance.

Teething

Timing

Lots of babies will start putting their hands and other objects in their mouths around three to four months, and dribbling lots. Exploring everything with their mouths is a huge part of their development in the first year – it's not necessarily teething.

Babies are born with twenty teeth developing in their gums. For lots of babies, these teeth will start to move in the gums around four months of age; most will find this uncomfortable. Babies might get their first teeth anywhere between six to twelve months and get the last somewhere between two to three years. They won't be teething for this whole time. Their teeth will move around and cut through for a few days at a time and then they'll settle down for a while until the next lot start moving.

To see what order they generally come in, do an internet search for 'Baby teething order of eruption'.

It doesn't matter if babies don't get their teeth in the traditional order.

Signs of teething

Teething babies will often be grizzly, red in the cheeks and gnawing on anything they can get their hands on. They might have a bit of a temperature, nappy rash or smelly (smellier) poo. When they are teething, they might have some sleep disruption and they might go off their food (either milk, solids or both). Fun times!

Remedies

1) Amber beads: a choking hazard, no evidence for their use

2) Teething gels: chat to your pharmacist about whether these would be appropriate for your baby

3) Analgesia such as Panadol or Nurofen: ask your pharmacist

4) Teething rings and baby rusks: something for them to gnaw on, the pressure feels good.

Have a look at the Raising Children Network fact sheet: **http://raisingchildren.net.au/articles/dental_care_babies.html**

Teething is totally manageable if you're happy (and it is appropriate) to give your baby analgesia which, as a nurse, I totally was. Some kids get their teeth without a fuss anyway, if you're lucky!

Cleaning their teeth

Once your baby has a tooth, it's time to start cleaning it! Giving it a little scrub in the bath with a face washer and water will do the trick. No toothpaste until eighteen months old.

Most babies will have a few teeth by their first birthday. From a dental hygiene point of view, this is the age a dentist would recommend weaning off the bottle, sending your baby to bed with clean teeth and not drinking anything other than water through the night. Yes, milk can decay teeth!

From a practical point of view, lots of little ones continue to love their bottle or even need an overnight feed after this time. A good compromise is to give an evening bottle, then clean their teeth.

Visiting the dentist

There's no need to go to the dentist in the early years to have your baby's teeth checked unless you have concerns about their dental health. As long as you look after them, you can wait until they are in pre-school and capable of cooperating with the dentist during the check-up!

Safety

Yes, this is a bit of a dry topic but, for once in your life, it's probably time to take it seriously, as your child's health and safety is obviously of paramount importance to you.

I think a good way to start thinking about this topic is by looking at the most common cause of injury and death for children in Australia. This will get you thinking about how these things might apply to you, your household and your child's environment and prompt you to work on any safety issues from there.

The most common causes of childhood injuries in Australia

1) Falls: for example, from change tables and beds

2) Poisoning: for example, by ingesting dishwashing liquid that is under the sink in the kitchen

3) Burns and scalds: for example, from a hot cup of coffee or a baby turning on the hot water in the bath

4) Drowning: for example, if you got distracted by your phone ringing while bathing the baby

5) Crushing: from a child climbing on furniture which topples on them

6) Choking: on a small toy, a hard piece of food or household item

7) Biting: by the family pet.

As you go about your day-to-day activities with your baby, have a think about what could be potentially dangerous as they grow and develop. Start putting in place changes, removing dangerous objects and choking hazards, adding safety locks and gates etc.

The Royal Children's Hospital Safety Centre is a wonderful resource and has a great checklist that takes you through each room in the house to make sure everything is safe. Check it out! **http://www.rch.org.au/uploadedFiles/Main/Content/safetycentre/120544%20Home%20Safety%20Checklist%20A4.pdf**

Baby CPR and first aid

All parents should learn basic first aid, choking management and children's CPR. There are plenty of affordable classes out there that cater for this. Check out your local council or children's hospital to find a course. Every family should have ambulance cover.

Fire safety

All families should have working smoke alarms, a fire extinguisher, a fire blanket and a fire safety plan. Have all your important documents in one place that's easy to grab. Have a designated person to get baby out of the house in an emergency.

Car safety

The crux of this topic can be found here: **http://www.kidsafe.com.au/crguidelines**

Be wary of borrowing car seats or buying second-hand ones that might be missing essential pieces.

There are a huge range of seats out there with a variety of price ranges and safety ratings. All price ranges have a number of seats to choose from that are rated highly for safety.

I found one in a department store for about $250 and looked up its safety rating here: **https://www.childcarseats.com.au/**

These days, it is encouraged to leave your little one rear-facing as long as possible until they can't fit in that direction anymore.

Car seats can be a little tricky to install. I would recommend getting it done professionally the first time while both you and your partner observe. Once you get used to it, you will be able to do it efficiently yourself. If you get stuck, most brands will have a video demonstration on YouTube.

Illness and when to seek medical assistance

If your child seems unwell and you are not sure whether you need to get him seen by a GP, you should be able to get some medical advice over the phone or online first. A good starting point might be Nurse On Call or your state's relevant Parent Help Line (see relevant numbers at the end of the book).

Look at, for example, the RCH website or Raising Children Network that will most likely have a concise, easy-to-understand fact sheet, for example the ones on fever in children, gastro in children and viral illness in children.

When do you go to the GP? If you are worried or your research has told you to go.

If you can't get to the GP, do you have a local home visiting GP service?

When do you go to the hospital? If your GP or parent phone line tells you to go.

When do you call an ambulance?

Call an ambulance when:

1) your baby is having difficulty breathing
2) they are semi-conscious or unconscious
3) your baby is very dehydrated
4) they have a prolonged seizure

5) they seriously burn themselves

6) they have a big knock to the head and are vomiting

7) the nurse on call tell you to

8) you feel very worried and your parental intuition tells you something is not right.

Emergency departments are chronically overloaded by children with health conditions that can be dealt with by a GP. Where appropriate, please try to see your GP first.

Leaving your baby in the care of others

Leaving your baby in the care of others can be an anxiety-inducing exercise for some parents. If it feels unnatural and uncomfortable, don't push yourself to do it. There's plenty of time for you to have time away from your baby. Some might tell you that you can't be a good parent unless you have 'time for yourself' but again, each to their own. If you find time away more stressful than rejuvenating, leave it for later.

I felt physically uncomfortable being away from Eliza in the early months. Later, when she was on the bottle, I enjoyed a bit of time away but mostly when Luke was looking after her in her own environment. We tried one futile sleepover with poor Nanna in the first year and haven't attempted it again.

Do what feels comfortable, not what you feel pressured to do. There's going to be plenty of time in the future for sleepovers. On the flip side, if you have someone you feel utterly comfortable leaving your child with and you feel okay being away from them, go! Enjoy yourself!

Going back to work

Lots of parents these days plan on going back to work after the birth of the baby. If this is going to be in your baby's first year or so, it's worth looking into childcare options when you're pregnant. There is certainly more demand than there is availability in many suburbs and wait lists can be upward of two years for popular centres.

Family members are great options, particularly for young babies. They are familiar, they are probably happy to come to your house and they will be emotionally invested in your child, attending to their needs promptly.

If your baby needs to go to day care below the age of two, I'd definitely recommend going and spending some time in the baby's room to make sure you are comfortable with the whole set-up. When I was pregnant with Eliza, I was sure I would send her to day care once I returned to work a year later. Once I had Eliza, was bonded and attached to her, my comfort levels with day care declined. There is nothing more stressful as a parent than leaving your child in a situation that neither of you feels comfortable with, so be well informed and prepared.

Alternatively, look into sharing a nanny with other parents or family day care, which is a childcare worker minding usually four children in her home. The children won't all be babies so they will have more time to have your baby on their hip through the day if need be.

Once you've organised your day care, give yourself and your baby a good period of time to slowly orientate to that environment in the lead-up to leaving them there for the full day.

To find all of your local childcare options and vacancies (other than a nanny), have a look at this website: https://www.careforkids.com.au

If you don't need to work, you don't need to send your child to day care for 'socialisation'. Catching up with your friends and family for play dates and doing activities like story time at the library and going to the park is enough 'socialisation' until they go to kindergarten. If you need a few hours' break, occasional care is a perfect option.

Childcare costs

Childcare costs vary depending on the postcode of the childcare you are looking at. From what I can grasp, the closer into the city centre, the more expensive the cost seems to be. The cost for a full day of day care might range from $80 per day to $150! How much of this you get back as a rebate depends on your family's income and will be discussed in the Centrelink section of the book. The rebate is capped at $7,500 a year, whether you use one day of childcare a week or five days, but this will change mid-2018.

Centrelink

I can't profess to have a perfect understanding of the whole of the Centrelink payments scheme but I'll go over the basics that apply to everyone. I must say, dealing with Centrelink is a headache for most people. If you persist with it, you'll get it done eventually. Be prepared, realistically, to spend a long time (thirty minutes plus) waiting for phone enquiries, website applications crashing and needing to physically go into the branch a couple of times.

Paid maternity leave

Many employers will pay you something while you're on maternity leave. Some will only give the time off but won't pay you anything, which is deplorable.

Your workplace should pay you your usual wage; lots of them will be happy to pay you at half pay for double the time. For example, if you are entitled to ten weeks' paid leave, you might choose to take twenty weeks of half pay. Ask your boss or HR department.

The paid parental leave from Centrelink is paid at the minimum wage for eighteen weeks.

If you are lucky, you can take your paid maternity leave from your workplace and, once this has finished, move over to Centrelink payments for eighteen weeks.

What to apply for?

You can choose to apply for a number of things, including paid parental leave, childcare rebate, childcare benefit and Family Tax Benefits A and B.

Paid parental leave is means-tested and available to mothers with an income less than $150,000 a year.

Partner leave is also means-tested, available for partners with an income of less than $150,000 a year and is paid at the rate of minimum wage for two weeks. Your partner would have to take unpaid leave from work to be entitled to it.

On top of paid parental leave, once you are the care giver to a dependant child, you may be eligible for an ongoing Centrelink payment called the Family Tax Benefit Parts A and B. These are paid depending on your social situation and family income; for example, being a single parent or having a low combined family income.

If your child has a disability, you will need to speak to your health care provider about extra payments you might be entitled to.

Making your application

When you have your baby, the hospital will provide you with a Centrelink form that is your proof you've had a baby.

You can do your application online on the 'myGov' website: https://my.gov.au/mygov/content/html/about.html

To start your application, you'll need the hospital paperwork as well as your and your partner's incomes and tax file numbers (TFNs).

When you submit your application online, you generally

won't hear anything for weeks. I'd give a courtesy call after a couple of weeks to check they have your application and if there's anything else they need from you for them to process it. They may be able to tell you your baby's Medicare number and both of your Client Record Numbers, which will be useful to jot down.

I wouldn't bother doing your childcare application until you know when you're going back to work and exactly what your wage will be, as this will affect how much rebate you will be entitled to.

If you are relying on Centrelink payments the week the baby is born, submit your application for paid parental leave and family benefits A and B when you are pregnant and then submit your proof of birth when the baby is born via the myGov app. Otherwise, organise your paid parental leave from your workplace to begin with and do the Centrelink stuff once the baby is born.

For the Centrelink paid parental leave, you need to let Centrelink know when you expect to start getting payments from them. Sometimes Centrelink will organise to pay the money to your employer who will continue to make your payments for the eighteen weeks of minimum wage. Check with your employer, as this part is a little confusing!

Childcare rebate

Childcare rebate is available to everyone and covers up to 50% of your out-of-pocket childcare expenses up to an annual limit of $7,500 per child.

Childcare benefit is an extra rebate off your daily childcare costs and is means-tested based on your family's combined income. For example, based on Luke's and my combined incomes at the time, I was entitled to an extra 22% off my childcare cost.

When you know when you are going back to work, how many days you will be working and what your wage will be, you can go back into the myGov website and apply for the childcare rebate and your childcare benefit.

In July 2018, all of the childcare rebates will be rolled into one simpler rebate called the Childcare Subsidy. Families earning less than $185,710 a year will no longer be subject to a cap on the amount of subsidy they can access. This will make sending your child to childcare more than two days a week much more affordable.

Clear as mud? Good luck with that!

Your better life as a parent

The absolutely best thing about becoming a modern-day parent is that it puts things in your life into perspective. Gone are the days of feeling stressed about social status, fashion trends and world travel. Hello to the days where what really matters is that you have a healthy, happy child and family. I have found so much peace in this new perspective.

Want another designer bag? You'd rather save that money for your child's education (#enlightenment).

Expensive dinners and holidays? A night in with your little family reading books and dancing to the Wiggles will be what makes you happiest (#netflixandchillplusbaby).

Need support? Real friends, step up (#buildingthevillage)!

Birthdays? All of a sudden, you want to spend them with your family again (#familyiseverything).

What's happening in the world? You'll really start to see how lucky we are to live in a peaceful country where we are safe, housed, fed and educated (#theluckycountry).

Reflection

Whilst I reflect on my first year as a parent and prepare to bring another baby into our lives, my most overwhelming feeling is that I hope I can relax and enjoy this baby more. While stressing about things I had very little control over, I feel I missed out on a lot of enjoyment that was there to be had in Eliza's first year.

Our next baby will be our last baby and I hope to savour every up and down. Wouldn't it be great if every first-time parent could parent like it was their *last* baby?

I think the key for me will be learning to go with the flow a bit more, learning to roll with the punches and not let the sleepless nights and parenting fails get in the way of the pure joy of that new life. This too shall pass. Every stage will have its difficulties. Every stage will be beautiful.

If you have taken even one thing from this book that will heighten your enjoyment of your parenting experience, I am thrilled. One piece of information to make you feel more relaxed or that helps you better understand your baby – I am stoked. Given you some helpful resources or some tools to manage difficult periods – fantastic. Shown you that there is no right way to parent any child – essential! Empowered you and your family to feel like you are doing a great job and are the best person for that job – my absolute goal.

Thank you for taking the journey with me and remember…

WHATEVER WORKS!

THIS TOO SHALL PASS!

Parenting information helplines by state

Australian Capital Territory

Parentline ACT:

(02) 6287 3833, 9 am–5 pm, Monday to Friday (except public holidays)

New South Wales

Parent Line NSW:

1300 130 052, 9 am–9 pm, Monday to Friday; 4 pm–9 pm, Saturday

Karitane Careline:

1300 227 464, 12.30 pm–9 pm, Monday to Thursday; 9 am–3.30 pm, Friday to Sunday

Tresillian Parent Helpline:

1300 272 736 (1300 2Parent), 7 am–11 pm, 7 days

Tresillian live advice service, 5 pm–11pm, Monday to Friday

Northern Territory

Parentline Queensland and Northern Territory:

1300 301 300, 8 am–10 pm, 7 days

Queensland

Parentline Queensland and Northern Territory:

1300 301 300, 8 am–10 pm, 7 days

13 HEALTH:

13 43 25 84, speak to a registered nurse 24 hours 7 days, or request the Child Health Team 6.30 am–11 pm, 7 days.

South Australia

Parent Helpline South Australia:

1300 364 100, 7.15 am–9.15 pm, 7 days (calls outside these times will be redirected to the National Health Direct Helpline)

Tasmania

Parentline Tasmania:

1300 808 178, 24 hours, 7 days

Victoria

Parentline Victoria:

132 289, 8 am–12 am, 7 days

Maternal and Child Health Advisory Line:

132 229, 24 hours, 7 days

Western Australia

Grandcare (information service for grandparents):

1800 008 323, 10 am–3 pm, Monday to Friday

Ngala Helpline:

(08) 9368 9368 (metropolitan) or 1800 111 546 (regional callers), 8 am–8 pm, 7 days

Australia-wide helplines

National Breastfeeding Helpline:

1800 MUM 2 MUM (or 1800 686 268), 24 hours, 7 days

Perinatal Anxiety and Depression Australia (PANDA) Helpline: 1300 726 306, 9am–7.30 pm (AEST), Monday to Friday

Pregnancy, Birth and Baby: 1800 882 436, 7am-12am, 7 days

National Sexual Assault, Domestic and Family Violence Counselling Service:

1800 RESPECT/1800 737 732, 24 hours, 7 days

Summary of websites resources

Pregnancy care options

https://www.betterhealth.vic.gov.au/

Breastfeeding

https://www.breastfeeding.asn.au

http://www.lcanz.org/find-a-lactation-consultant/

http://raisingchildren.net.au/

Development

http://raisingchildren.net.au/

https://www.thewonderweeks.com

http://www.toylibraries.org.au/

Emotional wellbeing

http://www.panda.org.au/

www.mindthebump.org.au

http://howisdadgoing.org.au/

Domestic violence

https://www.1800respect.org.au/

Social

https://www.letsmush.com/

http://www.playgroup.org.au/

Sleep

https://lovetodream.com.au/

https://rednose.com.au/

Parenting advice

http://raisingchildren.net.au

Growth

http://www.education.vic.gov.au/childhood/parents/mch/Pages/charts.aspx

Immunisation

http://www.immunise.health.gov.au/

Introducing solid food

https://www.nhmrc.gov.au/_files_nhmrc/file/publications/170131_n56_infant_feeding_guidelines_summary.pdf

http://www.rch.org.au/

https://www.allergy.org.au/patients/allergy-prevention/ascia-guidelines-for-infant-feeding-and-allergy-prevention

Children's health information

http://www.rch.org.au/home/

http://raisingchildren.net.au/

Safety

https://www.rch.org.au/safetycentre/

https://www.childcarseats.com.au/

http://raisingchildren.net.au/articles/baby_slings_carriers_safety.html

Childcare

https://www.careforkids.com.au

Centrelink

https://my.gov.au/mygov/content/html/about.html

www.ingramcontent.com/pod-product-compliance
Lightning Source LLC
Chambersburg PA
CBHW071347080526
44587CB00017B/2999